EXIT!

First published by BlackBird Books,
an imprint of Jacana Media (Pty) Ltd
First, second and third impression 2016

10 Orange Street
Sunnyside
Auckland Park 2092
South Africa
+2711 628 3200
www.jacana.co.za

ISBN 978-1-928337-20-1

Cover design by Shawn Paikin
Set in Sabon 10/13pt
Printed and bound by Digital Action, Cape Town
Job no. 002856

Also available as an e-book:
d-PDF 978-1-928337-21-8
ePUB 978-1-928337-22-5
mobi file 978-1-928337-23-2

See a complete list of BlackBird Books titles at www.jacana.co.za

EXIT!

A true story

Grizelda Grootboom

BLACKBIRD
BOOKS

I wish to thank my mentor, Nozizwe Madlala-Routledge, a woman who has been a leader in the struggle for gender equality and human dignity for over 40 years. She has walked this journey of writing this book with me with humbleness and respect. I appreciate the time she has given to listen to me. I wish to thank her for starting Embrace Dignity, an NGO for women like us to be healed and recover our self-identity.

Prologue

I am Grizelda Grootboom.

I have survived a life of human trafficking.

I had a happy home until it was taken away from me; until my world fell apart.

After eighteen years of being trapped in the world of drugs and prostitution, I found an exit.

Now I am transforming: facing my traumas and feeling the pain after a life of physical abuse and emotional dryness; a life that lacked connection with anything meaningful, other than my drugs, my men. Prostitution.

I'm discovering wholesomeness. I'm proud of my growth, and I'm enjoying getting to know myself, taking care of myself. I can now call myself pretty.

I have a little son, S, I have promised him that I will try to make sure that he grows up in a healthy environment with love, proper caring and a sense of purpose.

This is my story.

PART 1

One

My life has seen cycles of abandonment and abuse, sexual exploitation and domestic violence. But my story begins long before I was born, because my mother was caught up in a similar cycle when she was a girl. We have together reflected on our respective experiences. But she doesn't know my whole story. Nor do I know hers.

These days I live with my mother and my son in Khayelitsha Site C, outside Cape Town. That's another cycle: it's the place where I was raped at age nine, where my disconnect with life started.

When I talk with my mother now, she doesn't give too much

detail about her life. We never really did talk about our family with each other. In fact, through the years of my childhood, we hardly had a relationship at all. Recently, once I had made my break from prostitution in Johannesburg and returned to a new life in Cape Town, I made a most notable discovery: that my mother, too, needs connection and healing.

She also wants to understand her past and what went wrong.

Hers is also a story of transformation, but not like mine.

She still prides herself on surviving without any education at all, leaving school in grade 1 and learning to support herself by buying and selling alcohol. It is no surprise that this attitude has replicated itself in my own survival strategies.

My mother was born in the early sixties in the coastal Eastern Cape, where she came to adopt Afrikaans as her language and Xhosa as her culture. She grew up as coloured because her mother was coloured, and she never knew her Xhosa father, who died when she was very young. She changed her Xhosa name as a way of changing her status during apartheid: the Cape was a 'Coloured Labour Preference' area, and being classified as coloured meant she could travel freely to Cape Town.

As a young teenager she travelled on her own to Cape Town. She tells me, 'I came to Cape Town and went to the docks, where I could find some work with the foreign sailors' clubs there. That's where I met your father, who lived with his grandparents in Woodstock. He also had his girlfriend, Joyce, there.'

My mother fell in love, but she never married my dad. As a result of that affair I was born on 7 December 1980, when my mother was nineteen years old.

When I was a baby, I was handed over to my dad, and I had a happy childhood.

I fondly remember growing up with my dad and his grandparents, Ouma Florie and Oupa David, who owned their vibrant Woodstock home on Roger Street. Their big green house with white trim was home to lots of friendly people: it bustled with the many foreign sailors and dock workers my great-grandparents took in as renters, and who came to the house to enjoy Ouma Florie's delicious food.

I loved the wooden stoep at the entrance – I would sit with my neighbours and watch life go by. Or I would walk the long inside passage with its grey vinyl tiles to the huge kitchen, with its constant aromas from pots filled with meat stews and curries. Attached to the dining-room wall was a fold-out bed – this was where my dad slept. I usually slept with my great-grandparents on the floor in their room.

In the dining room, a musical carousel acted as a movable room divider; on it a golden lady doll holding an umbrella revolved to the music. I used to love listening to this chime and watching the lady dance stiffly in an eternal circle. And I loved being with my dad, who would walk with me hand-in-hand singing his special song for me:

'I will be so lucky,
Lucky, lucky, lucky
I will be so lucky lips.'

My dad also had full pink lips, like me, and the Marvin Gaye-type hairstyle so popular in those days. I remember his brown eyes, and his false front teeth, one of which had a gold star on it. His narrow, moustached face lit up when he laughed.

Ginger, our fat cat, was usually curled up on the squeaky cane rocking chair with its stuffed green cushions that Ouma Florie had made. But sometimes Ginger and I would sneak under my dad's fold-out bed and spend the night listening to him having sex with his different girlfriends.

Joyce was my dad's long-time girlfriend. She was devoted to my dad, although he did things behind her back. When my dad wasn't around, Joyce usually was, and she spent a lot of time with me. She and Ouma Florie were like mothers to me – the only mothers I had ever known. An auntie lived with us too, but she wasn't interested in hanging out with me.

I didn't really know my mother in these early years. The first time I met her, I felt like she was just a relative, it did not feel like she was my mother. I have a vague memory of her visiting us in Woodstock, but she already had two other children by then. I remember sitting eating with them in the passage. And then they left. We had had no connection. And no one in Woodstock ever took the time to tell me much about her.

My dad didn't have a steady job, but would come and go from the house. Sometimes, he would disappear for several days. When he left the house without me, I enjoyed the smell of his deodorant, which lingered day and night.

I always knew when my dad was awake and at home because of the noise he made in the backyard toilet. I could hear his newspaper rustling – my dad used newspaper to wipe his bum. I would wait for him to emerge from the toilet, though sometimes this took hours. I knew he was done when I no longer heard the rustle of the paper.

Once he'd seen me, I'd ask, 'What are we going to do today?'

He'd normally mumble something, put on his Levi's jeans and Dr. Martens, and take me for a walk. We always enjoyed our time together.

Because Ouma Florie's house entertained lots of people,

and because she enjoyed cooking for them, her wooden stove was always loaded with boiling pots for the workers after their hard day's work. When Ouma Florie was in the kitchen, I knew the house would be packed with people feasting. There was an amazing feeling of peace when she was in the kitchen, even though the rest of the house was so noisy and joyful.

Every day when I arrived home from school, I would run down the long passage, skipping all the way to the kitchen at the back to greet Ouma Florie and hug her apron-clad waist. There was often a particular smell in the air – crayfish. Ouma would scare me by swinging live writhing crayfish in my face before putting them into boiling water. My screams usually caused laughter to break out among the onlookers in the kitchen.

My mother would send Ouma Florie some of the money she had earned, sometimes a whole box of coins. Then Oupa David would take it to his 'bank'. I spent a lot of time with Oupa.

Oupa David liked to bet on horses, so together we'd walk down to a betting house where old men, dressed in their suits with ruffled ties, would hustle and bet, and point their fingers in the air when they won. Oupa was dark-skinned, with a clean-shaven head. His strong, thick hands held mine gently but firmly during our walks to the betting house.

I was always excited when Oupa won a bet, because I knew I would be getting a toffee apple or an ice cream. And he didn't seem to mind my hands sticky with the toffee apple, ice cream and Viennas he would buy me. Grasping my hand every second, he would drink out of a brown-paper bag, make jokes and stumble back home, and I felt happy and safe when I was with him. I would come home sometimes still pulling toffee from my front teeth.

When he didn't have his brown-paper bag, Oupa stayed in his room and didn't socialise much. Sometimes, when he drank his tea, he would show me that he didn't have any teeth in his mouth.

But when my dad's brother, Donald, came to the betting house with Oupa and me, he spoilt everything. I was very talkative, and Donald would smirk at me and say, 'He's only buying you that so your teeth get sticky and you shut up' or 'Don't you disturb David when he's trying to bet on the horses.'

Donald was so annoying. Before school in the mornings, Donald would give me bitter orange jam with chilli on my bread, which I hated. But being taken to school with him was even more of a disaster.

Donald was a drag queen. Dressed in ladies' overalls like they used to wear in District Six, with the three hair rollers on top of his head tied with a scarf, he would walk me to Chapel Street Primary School, a few blocks away. His pink high heels with fur on top would click-click-click along the street.

As we rounded the corner of Roger and Chapel streets, all the kids would be waiting and laughing, shouting out: 'Oh, Grizelda! Uncle Moffie is back!' As he walked me into my classroom, he'd make the vulgar retort, '*Ek sal vir you ma sê.*' My school days were like that: the kids were cruel to both of us, but it was me who ended up crying from all the drama.

I soon learnt that Saturdays were good days to get back at him.

On Friday nights Donald wore dresses because he went to drag parties. And when he returned home early on Saturday mornings, he'd knock at the locked front door. I was the only one who would notice, peaking at him through the letter opening.

Left outside, he would eventually pass out on our stoep.

Every week it was the same.

So on Friday afternoons, I would find a flying cockroach, catch it and put it in a bottle. On Saturday mornings, while he was still asleep on the stoep, I would take the roach out of the bottle and shove it in his weave. Later, Ouma Florie would throw something at him, startling him out of his drunken sleep. That's when Donald would jump up with his high-pitched cry, 'Oooh, I've got a cockroach in my hair!' He'd run down the road in his drag-queen dress, waking up the sleeping community of Roger Street.

Of course my dad would be asleep in the dining room with Joyce. So I would watch from the window and laugh and laugh.

One time I woke up early on a Saturday morning and, peeking through the letter opening of the front door, I saw Donald slouched and snoring in the cane chair, wearing a white wedding dress! I ran back to Ouma, woke her up and told her. We thought he'd got married!

She took an ash tray made from a rubber tyre, opened the front door and threw it straight at Donald's head. Startled, and letting out a loud whimper, he jumped up and ran out of the house and down the street, his white wedding dress fluffing around him, crying, 'Oh, oh. Help! Ouma's throwing things at me!'

This caused a huge stir the neighbourhood – everyone was watching and laughing. But I think I laughed the loudest of all!

Sundays meant a lot to me. Ouma would give me nice oats for breakfast, then dress me up for church in my white dress with white clicky shoes.

Although she would walk me to church, she never attended herself – she loved cooking and would be wanting to go home to prepare our huge Sunday lunch. Everyone knew that by 11am, the aromas from your kitchen needed to have reached the street – that was how we always knew what our neighbours would be eating.

I really loved those days.

When I returned home, I would change out of my white dress, happy to see Ouma's perfect lunch waiting for me: grilled potatoes, chicken with yellow rice, and squash. Silma, my Muslim friend from next door, and I would sit on the stoep swopping our dishes when our parents weren't watching. I loved her chicken biryani and she loved my Ouma's squash with its pool of melted Rama.

I'd eat with my own metal spoon, which had flowers elegantly etched on it. After our lunch on the stoep, Silma and I would eat a dessert of canned mixed fruit with green jelly and custard in our little bowls.

We'd watch the people walking by, the kids skipping rope in the street, the guys doing their break dancing. And we'd chat and laugh about Donald. In those days Donald was hanging out with this guy called MJ (after Michael Jackson) – a guy who always wore a black leather jacket and white shirt, and who thought he was going to meet the real Michael Jackson some day. Donald, dressed in his ladies' overalls, would stand close to MJ, twisting his curly hair in his fingers. Silma and I laughed so much at them, mimicking them and wondering what made Donald want to play with MJ's hair.

Oh, the streets were alive, and it was a fun community. On those relaxing Sundays, everyone went about their own friendly business, talking with neighbours all day. And I was a kid like any other, and my home was a happy one. Outside, in Roger

Street, people listened to radio songs, drank and danced wildly in the streets, and this often went on through the night, though nobody complained of any noise. I remember my auntie singing songs from the radio, sometimes Judy Boucher, which was very popular then. She had a beautiful voice, and she was funny when she'd had a bit to drink.

This was my home; I felt safe and happy.

Two

I WAS EIGHT YEARS OLD when things began to fall apart.

It started when our beloved cat, Ginger, who I cared for so much, became pregnant. Ginger was my closest friend, a cat who purred (or rather snored) me to sleep each night.

When I came home from school one afternoon, I found out that Donald had put Ginger in a black plastic bag and thrown her away in the Woodstock garden, never to be seen again. After that, I went back to the gardens many times hoping to find her – at first I looked all over, but after a few times I would just sit on a bench hoping to see her again.

If I'd been irritated by Donald before, I hated him after that. I never really spoke to him again, except when I had to.

Just after that Donald told Joyce about my dad's other sexual exploits. I remember the way she took this news: she was hysterical. She ran outside to the backyard toilet and tried to commit suicide by taking a handful of tablets.

I remember standing next to her, staring at the pills in her hand. I told her how sad I was about Ginger, and I said that I wanted to take a pill as well.

Joyce didn't take the pills that day, and I sat with her as she calmed down. But she left Roger Street after that, and I never saw her again.

And oh, I was traumatised about Ginger. I cried for days on end. Donald had killed my dear cat, and I didn't understand why.

So that's how my sadness began.

One day, shortly thereafter, Oupa David left the house wearing a light-tan suit, and never came home.

No one told me what had happened. I kept asking where Oupa David was, and nobody told me.

On the day of his funeral, I was told to come with, and I still had no idea what was happening or why. I hid in Oupa's bedroom, among his clothes, and I didn't come out. I really thought he would come back. Eventually, Donald said they should leave without me. And they did. It was only years later that I found out that a car accident had ended his life.

After that, Ouma Florie went very still, like a ghost. She became tired and depressed. I don't think she ever recovered from the shock of his death. There was no cooking, and for the first time that I could remember, the house was quiet.

A few months after Oupa David died, Ouma Florie passed

away. She had a heart attack, I was told.

And then my dad got really depressed. He'd lost his grandparents who had always loved and supported him, and he'd lost Joyce. My dad got more drunk, more often, and he started leaving the house even more.

And then another rock hit.

My dad learnt that we had to leave the Roger Street house because the buildings in the area were scheduled for demolition. The government planned to construct new flats, which we were told to apply for. My dad didn't bother though: he didn't have a job, and thought he wouldn't qualify for housing. He couldn't have paid any rent anyway. He was too lost by then to even attend the community meeting at St Philip's Church.

Things were going from bad to worse.

My sadness was growing. I was confused about having to leave home, but I thought that when we moved, I would stay with my dad. Because we *belonged* together.

But in those last few weeks at home in Roger Street, I didn't know where he was most of the time, and I missed him.

And it was around then that he told me he couldn't take care of me any more. I was so hurt. I was sure he was lying; that he just didn't want to take responsibility for me.

I remember him taking me to look for my mother at the docks nearby, thinking she was still living there. He'd heard she was living with a new husband in an abandoned boat in the shipyard.

Several times we went there together. Several times he left me sitting for hours on a bollard that the boats were tied to, and I would swing my legs, eating my fish and chips carefully wrapped in paper, waiting for my mother to pick me up, like he'd said she would, or for my dad to return ...

Nobody came.

Just the seagulls circling to steal my chips.

Each time, late in the day, one of the fishermen who'd stayed at our house would recognise me and bring me home to Roger Street where all around us the demolitions were starting.

This was my dad's way of dumping me, though I didn't know it at the time. There was weeks of this, and eventually the demolitions forced us out of our home in Roger Street. I don't know where my auntie or Donald went.

After we left Roger Street, my dad found a shelter for us to stay in near the docks. We spent the next two nights there, the two of us. But I think he just tried to find somewhere safe to leave me. Because one day when I was at the shelter, he left for the day and never came back.

At eight years old, I had been abandoned.

I only knew one route to walk. I knew the way from the Roger Street house to the docks, and from there to the shelter. I walked that route, looking for my dad. I kept going back home, kept going back to Roger Street, although there was no one there any more. And every time I went back, the house was more broken down.

The shelter, the street and my broken home, the street, the shelter – that was the circle I would walk. Trying to find home. Trying to put the pieces back together again.

Trying to find my dad.

But with the house gone, it was like he had disappeared.

You had to pay to sleep in the shelter in those days. My dad had paid for just a few nights for me, and then my time was up. At the shelter, I met some kids, kids who knew the streets, who knew about life at the docks. Many of them lived under the bridge near the Gallows Hill Traffic Department in Green Point, and that is how I came to live under the bridge too – my home, on and off, for the next few years.

I wasn't in school any more – how could I be? I spent a lot of time moving, roaming, searching. I met Donald again that way, since he was now living at the docks. We bumped into each other. He was still a drag queen, mostly always drunk and trying to survive in his own way, but the one thing about Donald was that he knew where the family was. He knew how to get information from the dock workers.

So it was Donald who found out where my mother was, where she lived with her own family. He told me to go look for her in Site C, Khayelitsha.

I didn't know where to go, nor did I speak any isiXhosa. There was no one I could ask. I took the train to Khayelitsha, but I was too scared to get off there, so I returned to Roger Street to sit and hope, and then back to the bridge.

I made that aborted journey again and again.

Eventually I found my mom.

I was nine when I joined her, her husband, Richard, and their two sons, Brendan and Owen, in Khayelitsha.

I hardly knew my mom, but my expectation was that she would be happy to see me, that she would be nice to me and take care of me. She would see that I needed someone to take care of me. I was just a little child. But when I met her again, she was like a stranger.

It all turned around.

My mother had been happy without me. She was now respectably married, with her own life and family. She worked as a sales lady in a Muslim-owned furniture store in Kwa Trek, a shopping mall in nearby Mandalay.

There was shame I put on her from the first moment I arrived. She didn't want to 'look bad' because she had a fatherless child, so she really didn't want me there. She kept asking me if I'd found my dad, and she beat me when I said no.

She told her husband I was her brother's child.

I had no friends in my mom's house. My two half-brothers didn't care about this Afrikaans-speaking 'relative'. They considered me a bit of a reject and made life difficult for me. They were only a few years younger than me.

I looked at them and thought they had a great life. Their father, Richard, was a truck driver, and he came back from a trip just after I arrived, bringing them new clothes and sweets.

Richard wasn't happy about me being around either. He never tried anything with me, but when she was at work, I could feel his eyes following me.

And the sandy, windy township was so strange compared to the suburb of Woodstock with its proper roads and shops, churches and schools and old brick houses. When I moved to Khayelitsha, shacks were being built and people were painting them to try and make them look good.

You'd hear koof-koof-koof in the middle of the night: people arriving from the Eastern Cape, building their shacks. Dogs barking, sand being moved. The more houses that went up, the more sand was dumped in the road, which had to be shovelled.

The language of the community was isiXhosa, and it sounded strange to me. I soon realised that the culture here was very different to what I was used to. When I settled into my mom's Khayelitsha home, people would ask me where my mother was because my mother continued to tell people in the community that I was not her daughter. As a child, I didn't know what to say. In my head, I would say, 'My mother is here.' But I knew my mother had told the community something else, so I just shut up.

The young girls who lived around us were also curious to know who I was – I didn't speak isiXhosa, yet I looked like them. I had a massive Afro because my granny had always allowed it to grow – she used to plait my hair. My mother didn't like my hair. This was not my home.

I remained in the back, outcast.

I had imagined that once I was with my mom, I would go straight back to school. But my mother seemed to take her time putting me into school. Instead, she got me to do labour around the house. And she would get angry when she thought I wasn't cleaning the house well enough.

My mother had always been industrious, always a survivor, and so, on Saturdays, besides selling alcohol, she held a 'Chinese cinema' at the house, using a cloth and projector. She charged 50 cents per person, and a lot of kids came because they didn't have television in their houses.

And when I arrived, the family gained a cleaner. Every day I had to walk and collect water from a communal tap far away and do chores in the house. The only benefit of my water-fetching was that I got to go outside. I met people and began recognising people and making friends. Gradually, over those first few days, I started to understand isiXhosa.

But life in my mom's house soon became like hell. My mother kept a half-jack bottle of Smirnoff vodka in her purse when she went to work, and there was a lot of drinking in the house. When Richard returned from his driving trip, he got angry and beat her up. When he left for his next trip, she took out her frustration on me.

I saw a lot of violence in that household.

Every day when my mother went to work, she would leave me with my duties for the day. She would tell me to go buy meat in Kwa Trek, and then come home and cook *umngqusho* (samp and beans). The first time, since I didn't know isiXhosa, I had to find somebody who could tell me how to get there.

In that house, cooking and cleaning had become my enslavement. I didn't mind the cleaning so much, but I minded the way my mother was treating me. She chastised me for not knowing how to keep sand out of the house. Sand became my curse. I had come from living in town, where there were roads, concrete and brick buildings and gardens. Now, the cursed sands of the township forced me into sweeping the same area sometime three times an hour, just to keep my mother quiet.

Sometimes, she'd tell me to 'spring clean' before her husband came home from a driving trip. And when he did, without warning, I'd be woken up in the middle of the night to make tea, *amagwinya*, steam bread, anything.

There seemed no possibility of going to school, but I had learnt to write in my Chapel Street Primary School in Woodstock. My unhappiness pushed me to start writing a diary about my little life, which I kept in the bag that I travelled around with. My mother didn't like me writing in my diary; it made her angry that I was wasting time when I could have been cleaning.

One day, when she sent me to Kwa Trek to buy chicken feet, she told me to find a barber and get my hair cut while I was there. This was a very sad moment for me. I had always loved my hair – I felt that I was myself because of my Afro. The other isiXhosa girls around seemed to like it, and I felt happy when they asked me if it was my real hair. It made me feel proud and important for a little while.

I cried while the guy cut my hair.

I asked myself why my mother was so vicious. Was it just that she was jealous of my big, fluffy Afro? I was being forced to be a Xhosa girl, as much as I didn't want to be.

It was on that same afternoon that I went to buy the chicken feet in Kwa Trek that I realised how much my mother was using me. Walking from my mom's house to the barber I could see the school. When I left the barber, feeling so hollow at the loss of my hair, I had to walk past the school again to get to Kwa Trek.

When was I going to go to this school like the other kids? I wondered. I felt like I was being treated differently and I didn't know what I had done to deserve it.

When I got to the furniture store, my mother didn't bother to introduce me to the boss. She just told to me how to prepare the chicken feet when I got home: how to boil the water, remove the dirt, skin and hair on the feet, and add beef stock. She instructed me to have the chicken-feet stew ready to eat by the time she got home from work – oh, and to make pap to go with it.

I was being kicked around and treated like a worthless being. I was waking up every day at 4am to make coffee and porridge for my mother and her husband, two people who didn't care a thing about me.

I'd been told I was worthless twenty-four/seven, ever since I had arrived. I realised then that all my mother could offer me was a place to stay sometimes – this was not a family I could be part of. I stayed only for about two weeks. I went back to living under the bridge with the other street kids.

After a while, I thought I should go back to my mom's house, to see if anything had changed. I remember arriving at her home; she was sitting inside the house on this big comfortable chair. She sat with an air of authority but she didn't act surprised when I showed up. It was more like she was waiting for an explanation. I had hidden my diary in the suitcase with my half-brother's clothes, and she'd found it and read it.

'You're back in my house,' she said to me, 'but you wrote all this stuff about me. So what do you want?'

She threw my diary in the fire. I watched it burn.

Then my half-brother Brendan and her husband Richard came out with a sjambok. I took the beating because I knew I wouldn't be able to run and catch the next train to town. After she beat me, I didn't even cry. After ten minutes, she commanded me to come help cook and clean up the kitchen.

All the time I was thinking about tomorrow: I would wake up, steal the R50 note I had seen inside, take a Coke, eat all the meat, and leave.

I was so tired of this woman. I was so angry with my mom. And so I became movable like the sand I was forced to sweep – leaving my mom, going back to Roger Street, back to the bridge, back to my mom. And every time I came back to Site C, she would beat me up.

Over and over again.

Like the sand, my sadness just kept coming back.

Three

By the time of my third stay in Khayelitsha, I had learnt basic isiXhosa greetings, and had slowly got used to the culture of Site C. At my mom's house I was spending most of my time cleaning and cooking, but by now I knew the routine in the house, and I had a plan for how to deal with my mom.

When she came into the house after work, I would grab the bucket and casually walk out so I could say I was going to get water. I knew she would have seen how the long queue at the tap was when she was walking back, and I could guess how much time I had before I needed to be home with the water.

Then I would ask the people in the queue to move my bucket along the queue – that is how I made time to play.

By then I had some friends there, three girls who lived around us. We girls used to play games after they came back from school and while I was fetching water for my mom, games like '*iThoti ezintathu*'.

To play '*iThoti ezintathu*' you line up three cans in the middle of a circle drawn on the ground, and two teams stand on either side. One team tries to hit the cans with a ball, and then the other team catches the ball on their side. After someone hits the cans, they run into the circle to put the cans up again, and the people on the other team try to hit that person with the ball. You have to dodge the balls at the same time as lining up the cans again.

When you see that kind of game being played close to a tap, and you're nine years old, you're going to want to join in! My new friends and I were all between nine and twelve, and we'd play in the time I had stolen while my bucket was in the tap queue.

I loved playing this game and the girls I played with quickly became good friends. I didn't have to worry about speaking good isiXhosa with them because they wanted to speak English, of which I knew a little.

But we weren't the only people playing games.

'*Efoli*' was a common game among tough gangster boys in the community.

It means 'get raped'.

One day it got late as we were playing near the tap. As it got darker, the streets got emptier, but it wasn't dark yet – just dusk, when the house lights are on and the moon is just rising.

Some of the boys in the community where watching us from nearby. They were about sixteen years old. One of my new girlfriends, the oldest one, who was twelve, knew one of these guys. She kept looking over at him.

'Hey, *sana*,' the guys yelled out.

'*Hayi, suka*,' we replied.

Would anyone watching have thought that we were trying to attract these boys with our childish game?

But the four guys strolled over, and casually put a knife to the oldest girl's side, and to us she said, '*Masihambeni*' (let's go). We knew she was thinking that if we didn't go with her they would stab her and run away.

She was asking us for help.

So we went to her.

The other guys surrounded us and jostled us down the street, making it look like we were walking together.

Now I too could feel the sharpness of the knife.

They forced us to walk the long distance to an empty shack near the community clinic. When we asked why they were doing this, they told us to shut up. Then we got kicked in the stomach and shoved inside the shack.

The oldest girl was first. She was put in another room.

While she was in there with one of the boys, the other three boys sat with the rest of us, waiting for their turn.

Four small girls, each raped, in turns, by four big boys.

When one boy finished, the next boy would enter the room and rape the girl again. The thing that was strange to me was that the first girl didn't scream. Where we sat waiting, if we screamed in fear, we got slapped. So we ended up staying quiet.

They released the girls one by one, once they had finished.

I was the youngest. I was the last.

I was terrified and in pain.

They are on top of me.

They all came into the room at the end.

There were all these legs around me, and sperm on my face.

Then they let me go.

It was a long walk home.

I was clutching my skirt between my legs and there was blood streaming down my legs.

The thing I remember is that there was a neighbour watching me as I walked all the way down the street to my mother's house. She was also a mother, and I knew her. She had smiled at me sometimes before when she had seen me playing at the tap – when she smiled I thought that she had felt happy for me, happy to see me adapting. But that night she just stared at me. And I felt blame and judgement. Her look made me feel shameful.

When you're out at that time, it's like you asked for it.

When I arrived home, my mother was drunk and ready with a sjambok. Hitting me, she asked me why I hadn't brought back the water and cooked dinner. Her sons had already eaten their sheep's head.

She beat me all over.

She never asked me where I had been. I kept quiet, and when it was over I went to clean the plates. I didn't eat supper, just licked the plates with leftover gravy still on it.

I was so angry with my mom. This was the final moment – I knew I had to leave this place. All I could think about was getting back to my dad.

In the next few days, the playing came to an abrupt end. At

the tap we girls ignored each other.

Ice cold.

We couldn't even meet each other's eyes.

For me, not knowing isiXhosa so well, it was all about the body language. Now it was the girls' body language and the look in their eyes that told me our brief friendship was over. So we never spoke or played together again. I guess we felt that if ever we spoke about our rape, something bad would happen to us, someone would harm us. It was partly the shock, but it was also the girls not wanting to bring shame to their families.

We just stayed afraid.

We knew that our community and parents wouldn't care. The community knew this happened regularly. No big deal. So we girls just split from each other.

After our ordeal, one of the girls got pregnant. She stayed inside her house, and we only saw her a few times after that when she came out to fetch water. A few months later, to avoid embarrassment, her family sent her back home to the Eastern Cape to have her child there. She was ten years old.

In the time to come, when I heard that the '*efoli*' boys had attacked some other girls too, I kept quiet, never telling anyone about my experience. Even now, communities protect the boys and young men who commit these crimes. But they don't protect their daughters. Blame is still cast on the girl for 'misbehaving'.

These cocky '*efoli*' boys continued their rampages. They would wait to catch the girls to 'play' with after school. They bragged about their various exploits. As time went on, they got bigger, stronger and more violent, and began hijacking cars. No one was really settled in Khayelitsha then: people were still taking over the land, minding their own business and building their shacks, and there wasn't much leadership. These vicious, arrogant boys ruled the township.

At the age of nine, to me all this suffering felt like a huge plot to ruin my life.

Everything was taken away from me when I was raped.

Looking back, I think this gang rape introduced me to the idea of being the kind of female I became in order to survive – it introduced me to the feeling of being exploited because I am female. But then, it made no sense. Nothing in my life in Woodstock had prepared me for this.

Khayelitsha was not for me. Three days later I left.

I told myself I would hate men forever.

Four

So I left my mom.

For several years after that, I lived on the streets of Woodstock, searching the area and asking people if they knew my dad. I missed him so much and I needed to find him again. I thought he might be working at the docks, and so I returned again and again, hoping perhaps that someone there would know where he was living.

Somehow, I kept alive the fantasy that my dad still loved me and would care for me.

In the years to come I was rarely in school. Instead, I moved from one shelter to another, or slept with my friends under the bridge. Of course there were drugs there – we street kids planned our lives around weed and the glue that we sniffed. That's one of the things we used to survive.

It was there that I met Freckles; I was eleven years old when I first met him. He was much older than me, in his early twenties. When I arrived on the streets I didn't know him but everybody would tell me about him. He used to date the fresh girls, the new girls to the streets.

On the streets and in the shelters, all of us girls felt we needed to have a boyfriend on the street. This worked for us: if you didn't have a boyfriend, you were considered an outcast, and you were not strong, and you would not survive this street life. You had to be tough.

If you had a gangster boyfriend, then you were automatically a member of his gang. This meant there was gangster violence and competition even among the girls in the shelters. Girls would beat each other up, and proudly announce their gang: if yours was the 26s or the 28s or The Americans, you'd have to tell me what your gang stood for and how much authority it had. For our own protection, it was good to be able to say, 'I got a boyfriend and he's the leader of the 26s, so what do you want?'

I knew I needed that protection.

Bruno, my light-skinned, freckled boyfriend, whom I nicknamed 'Freckles', was in the 26s. He was my way of manoeuvring through the hustle within the shelter.

Our relationship had developed fully by the time I was twelve. That's when he began taking me seriously and protecting me on the streets. Although it was an off-and-on thing, our relationship lasted a long time; I didn't date anyone else for years. I took him as my shield and my protection. Because on the streets it was all about that: dating the greatest and strongest gangster meant you were protected even if he wasn't around.

I wasn't even a teenager yet, and I didn't have any sexual urge, just childish crushes and a cockiness at being able to flirt and play with the boys. The girls who dated these kind of guys had told me what to expect. They told me that Bruno would expect to have sex with me but that I could avoid that by giving blow jobs. I liked being with Freckles but I was still so raw from my rape experience in Khayelitsha. I told Freckles I was a virgin and he seemed to accept that.

So Freckles didn't shag me – he just played with my body, kissed me and made me give him blow jobs.

Freckles lived on the street, but he would get locked up in jail sometimes for a few months. Always when he came back from jail he'd come and look for me. He wanted me with him all the time. He'd come find me in the shelter and keep me to himself for two or three weeks because he needed that comfort.

After a few weeks on the street with him, I'd come back to the shelter, and get cleaned up. Sometimes he would come to the shelter every weekend and just take me out, by literally unscrewing the gate.

The mother caretakers weren't very protective: when they saw what was happening, they would just let me go. When he took me away with him, the shelter would always blame me for 'misbehaving'.

But I never felt like Freckles was doing anything wrong. Moving around with Freckles was always something that I wanted. Sometimes I was really, really happy to be out of the shelter, to have that freedom, and Freckles was my best friend on the streets.

As I moved around with him, he never did anything nasty to me. He acted tough on the outside all the time, but he had a tender side, at least towards me. I liked his green eyes as they stared at me.

Five

For many years, I moved around between shelters or slept on the streets, looking for my dad, and sometimes I went back to Khayelitsha.

In my mother's community, people knew I was a street kid because they saw me coming and going from my mom's house. As I grew into my teens, people assumed that I was already a prostitute. To me they wouldn't say anything. But they had a lot to say to my mother. In her own way, she would defend me. She'd say, 'Well at least she comes and brings food, you know.'

But this stigma stopped me from becoming part of the

community because people had already made up their minds about who I was. I felt that if I wanted to be part of any community, I would have to be far from those streets where people thought they knew me.

In 1993, when I was twelve years old, I got involved, like other young kids at the time, in a political rally in Khayelitsha in which Chris Hani spoke against violence.

We ran while singing freedom songs, with no shoes or socks, the sand soft under our feet. It was us kids making noise, singing as we made our way to the stadium, singing and running, and then we got to this wide open space – a gathering of people with faith and hope and spirit, looking forward to change.

And everyone was talking about Chris Hani, telling us kids who he was and what he stood for. We were there for the whole day, waiting to hear him, and it was the most talked-about thing.

When he eventually spoke, I loved his voice, his activism, his presence.

He was so encouraging towards everyone and everyone was so excited to see him. By the time we heard his speech, I was in love with this guy who stood up against the things that were hurtful and painful. I felt like he knew my personal pain.

I had been uncomfortable in the dusty township after my life in Woodstock, but Hani told us that we deserved equal rights. That even if you were removed from a house with a proper toilet and you had to come to this dusty place, you could still make it. You were still worthy.

It was one of those special moments, a real moment of connection, and an escape from my life into a place where the community felt like a family, and everyone felt like they belonged. We came back late in the night, still buzzing from the toyi-toyi.

After seeing Hani, it started to make sense why I felt so frustrated at my dad and my dislocation from our happy, solid Woodstock home. And not only that, because what I saw in Khayelitsha were these people living in the wind-blown sand. The roofs of their shacks were covered with holes so that the shacks filled with sand when the wind blew, and flooded when it rained.

From Hani's speech, I learnt about what apartheid in the country meant for black people. We wanted clean streets, enough water and electricity, and to get things right, for everyone.

This was a moment when I started to enjoy Xhosa culture. But I still didn't want to stay in dusty, sandy, dangerous Khayelitsha. I always went back to the bridge.

***

Lea was a short and petite, a sometimes feisty, sometimes quiet girl of about my age, with pronounced Khoisan features – a big bottom, light skin and short, peppercorn hair. Her two front teeth were a discoloured yellow-brown, so she never had nice breath, no matter how much she brushed her teeth. She could be cheeky, but was loyal and she knew how to protect me. And I looked after her too – I always felt so protective of her, like she was my little sister.

Lea and I would often run away from the shelters and do our own thing on the streets with our boyfriends. We were both street kids, and we spent a lot of time together.

Both at the shelter and on the street, Lea became my very best friend. I trusted her to look after my toiletries during the times Freckles stole me away – so I trusted her with everything I had.

We were always getting caught by the police. They would catch us for stealing food from Shoprite, things like that. Usually, we'd get caught some time in the afternoon, and then we'd be locked up. The cops were always irritated by us being there, taking up space in the cells. They would spend a few hours scaring us.

In the evening, the shifts would change, and then the new cops would come in. They would tell us that they'd take us to Pollsmoor Prison unless we gave them blow jobs.

They'd all stand in a row together while we did that. Then the evening-shift cops would let us go.

It was the cops who took us to Ons Plek shelter, where I ended up staying, on and off, for most of my teenage years. Looking back, I know that Ons Plek gave me lots of opportunities.

But I hated it when I first arrived.

Ons Plek had three bedrooms, with six beds in each room. It looked like a prison. There were noisy wooden floors and you could hear what was going on above and below you.

And there were these tiny lockers, where we kept our stuff – clothes, toiletries, cigarettes, weed, glue, buttons (mandrax). We used to ask our gangster boyfriends to get us locks to put on our lockers, but still people were always breaking into them and stealing our stuff.

Like at all the shelters, it was survival of the fittest.

When I arrived I was already a cheeky, feisty bully. I arrived there together with Lea, straight from jail. On the first night there, we were split up and put in different bedrooms. I was very concerned about being split.

The next day midmorning, we were having a school lesson from these international volunteer tutors – they would come and try to teach us to read and write. Lea leant over and said to me that her vagina was burning. When she said that I looked at her neck, which was covered in love bites. I just knew that she'd been raped. On that first night there, Lea had been molested with sunlight soap.

I learnt later how this was done. The girls would spend the afternoon shaping the big green bar of soap into the shape of a penis, which they would use to rape new girls, girls who threatened the hierarchy of the tight group that formed in the shelter bedrooms.

I was so angry. There was no way the shelter mother couldn't have known what was going on – her room was right underneath the girls' bedroom with its noisy wooden floors.

We coped the only way we knew how – we kept quiet. But after that I refused to be separated from her. Every night I just went to her bed and slept there holding her while holding a knife tightly in my hand. If anybody tried anything they would have to go through me.

I was so angry. She was this tiny person. She was also such a quiet person – she didn't talk much about her life but you could see the sadness in her eyes. People always took advantage of her. I would have done what I needed to do to protect her.

These girls in the shelter, that was their home – and for most of them, it was the only home they'd ever had. We'd come without asking them, and they were protecting their territory.

I was used to the life in shelters, but Ons Plek was different because they gave me more than just bread and butter. They organised school for us. When we were injured, they'd take us to get medical care.

At the shelter we girls were very involved in the running of things. We had duties we had to do to get things done around the place. We cooked our own food. When it was our turn, we got up really early in the morning – we had to make mealiemeal porridge. But if you were the person cooking breakfast then your privilege was to shower first with hot water ... and maybe you'd purposefully finish it.

The kitchen duty gave you a time to feel like you were in control. You knew everybody in the house would want to be your friend because they wanted more food. And it gave you some authority – you had to watch that no one took too much food, but you had the control to give a little bit extra to the people you liked.

The other duties never had the same impact – it was always about food. We ate a lot of expired Woolworths food. The only meat we ate was turkey pieces for Saturday supper.

During that time in the shelters, I went to Jan Van Riebeeck Laerskool on Kloof Street in town, which I especially enjoyed. I was in a special class, with shorter hours, with kids of different nationalities who struggled with language and education. My teacher, Mrs Taylor, was great. I was slow to read and write, and she encouraged me so much.

I played netball and went to a lot of netball and rugby tournaments in the Western Cape. On the tournaments I got to know Matthew, a cute guy – I had such a crush on him. Sometimes it felt like I was only going to school just for him, to deliver the love letters that I was always writing him. He was kind, and I was always so surprised that he took my cards from me.

At that time I felt like I lived in two different worlds.

I was still leaving the shelter often: Freckles would come and get me for the weekend and sometimes I'd only come back by

Wednesday. But it was because of Matthew that I started going back to the shelter after every weekend – I needed to be at Ons Plek on Monday mornings so that I could get my uniform and go to school.

I never really knew how he felt about me, but at the school dance at the end of the year, I danced with him. Just the two of us in the near-empty hall, dancing to 'All for love' from *The Three Musketeers*.

That made me so happy.

Six

THERE WERE VOLUNTEERS WE KNEW from the church who used to bring food parcels to us when we were staying under the bridge. One day in 1995, a few of these volunteers came to collect us – they told us that we were going to go to Johannesburg for Madiba's birthday because he wanted to spend it with us.

Even though we didn't have families, there was a feeling among us that uTata took care of us. Every year on his birthday the shelters were given party packets and a huge birthday cake with Mandela's face on it from Pick n Pay. We always loved that – we really felt some connection to him. We'd sing happy birthday even though he wasn't in the room. I sometimes felt a bit stupid singing to someone who wasn't there, so I was happy I was usually high and could really celebrate these moments. They were the good times. It was so exciting, something we really enjoyed, which made us feel like he was looking after us.

I was fourteen when we Cape Town street kids were collected and flown to Joburg, to a hotel in Gold Reef City to meet Madiba. So this was something different – we were finally meeting uTata!

There we went from the streets of Cape Town to an expensive Joburg hotel. It was madness – we took over the hotel for about three days, smoking weed and glue, sometimes passing out. It was all very exciting: it was cool that we were getting the opportunity to see uTata, and it was cool to sleep in a clean bedroom, to not have to share a shower. We felt expensive, and important. And we felt spoilt, knowing it was uTata's money that was giving us this gift. For once we were not being punished for being street kids. And everything was clean. We were so excited we almost didn't sleep. We would wonder around the hotel wearing our sheets, pretending to be ghosts.

By the time we got to meet with Madiba, most of us were high on glue, and the social worker could only take the younger kids to meet Madiba up close. While Madiba was making his speech and talking about education, there we were at the back calling out and waving: '*Viva*, Madiba! We are so happy you are out now! *Viva*, Tata!'

By the time Madiba finished, we were already gone, back to Gold Reef City to swim and have fun.

The hotel was near a park. Some of the kids took off their

new Madiba T-shirts, and headed to the intersection to beg for money. They didn't want to return to Cape Town. Back in the hotel, I heard this rumour that they were going to run away. They had an opportunity to be in another city: and we all knew that the bigger the city, the more places there were to beg for money. These kids had no reason to stay in Cape Town.

I still regarded Cape Town as home though, so I was never tempted to stay in Joburg. I had my relationship with Freckles and I was getting used to going to school.

And there was my dad – I still wanted to find him.

On the day we left, the volunteer caretakers and shelter mothers looked for the rest of the kids, but we flew back to Cape Town with lots of empty seats on that plane.

When we got back to Cape Town, we knew Madiba's voice; we knew that in Cape Town the older street boys were paid R10 to put up posters of him. We also knew where De Klerk lived, and that Mandela had been in prison on Robben Island, which we could see beyond the docks.

We knew it was the end of apartheid, and the city itself was high.

But what did it all mean to *us*? We loved the Madiba T-shirts we were given. We would wash them, hang them out carefully, and sleep in them on the side of the road.

* * *

A few years before this what we street kids couldn't understand was why so many people had flocked to Cape Town's Grand Parade five days before Madiba's inauguration speech in May 1994. What were they all doing there on the streets, *our* streets, all these people from all over the world?

There were celebrations in town every day and suddenly

there were all these road blocks and we didn't understand – it sometimes irritated us because they were messing with our escape routes, the routes we normally took when we'd stolen something from Shoprite.

So we climbed the walls of the City Hall, and the library, and the clock tower, and sat in the shade, watching all these people.

We heard people yelling, 'Freedom!'

And we robbed the visitors, stealing their money and bags. By 2am every night, our sleeping quarters under the bridge would look like a frickin' Chinese shop! The next day, we would sell the bags and buy weed. It was an amazing time for us as we moved through the crowds.

We felt so free. Everyone was happy; no was was focused on us.

Our special treat was fish and chips – that was what we'd buy when we had earned more money than usual, which we did on those amazing days. If one of our guys was puzzled and asked, 'Who is this Mandela guy?', we'd tell him to shut up and just eat his fish and chips.

By the end of Madiba's inauguration speech, we had celebrated our freedom and were high on drugs.

PART 2

Seven

IN 1996, WHEN I WAS fifteen I was moved from Ons Plek shelter in town to Siviwe shelter in Woodstock, near Salt River Road. Siviwe was a more stable shelter – their main aim was to reunite street kids with their families. It was cleaner and had nicer facilities. I was moved there because the guardians felt I needed more stability.

It meant I was not living with Lea any more, but I saw her most Friday nights, when the Ons Plek girls and the Siviwe girls gathered together for a social time.

Siviwe ran a programme at the Salt River community centre

to get us kids involved in activities – painting or acting classes, and things like that. It was there that I bumped into my dad's brother Donald again. He was now an HIV activist working at the centre. I'd given up on Donald a long time before, and I didn't want a friendship with him now, but there was something he could tell me – he knew where my dad was.

I kept that information for a long time before I found the courage to go to my dad's house.

I kept my dad's address to myself until a certain Friday. When the new shelter mother arrived for her shift late in the day, I lied to her and told her that I'd already got permission to see my dad for the weekend. She gave me money for the train to go and to come back, and told me that I had to call the shelter when I got there.

I had planned to go on a Friday evening because I believed I would sleep at my dad's place. I thought he would happy to see me.

It was a weekend I lived to regret.

Extension 3A in Gugulethu. That's where I found my dad's house and learnt that he had set up a shebeen there with a new girlfriend, Beverly. They had one son, Storm.

My dad was high when I arrived. There was a feeling of resistance. I had always had so much hope that he would take me back. But he was now with Beverley, and he was cold towards me. I felt it deeply. It was clear that they didn't want me to stay there. I think my dad had the same attitude as my mom: that if I stayed with him, I would mess up his family life with Beverly.

We ate together that night, but as time passed I felt that he needed to go somewhere and that I needed to leave. He made it sound like he'd always known where I was. He said he'd come visit me at the shelter.

And then my dad left.

I couldn't travel back to the shelter so late on a Fiday night – it's dangerous travelling alone on trains, especially at night. So I decided to hang around in Gugulethu. I smelt some weed and followed the smell to a house where some guys were smoking. They let me sleep there.

My dad's house was not far from the house of the singer Ringo Madlingozi. The next morning, I sat for a while and listened to him playing his music in front of the Rasta vegetarian shop.

When I went back to the house, I met Beverly and Storm. Beverly was angry with me. She locked the house and told me I must wait outside. And then she also left. I don't know what happened. I waited the whole day, until it was very late, and no one came back.

I got the picture – I was not wanted.

Even though it was already dark, I decided to back to town, to spend the rest of the weekend under the bridge. Then I could return to Siviwe and pretend it had all gone OK.

I was raped on the train coming back.

I could not fight my attacker. Rather raped than killed, I thought. I never told anyone what happened on the train coming back from my dad's house. The only person I felt I could relate to was Lea.

At Siviwe, I started misbehaving, and so I was moved back to Ons Plek. I'd be there for a few months and then I'd be sent back to Siviwe, where I still had a bed. They kept my bed because they felt there was hope for me, that I was just going through a bad patch.

But the pain of my dad not wanting me pushed me right back. He had a home – why didn't he want me there? I was once his child ... and now he has another family? How in the hell does that happen so quickly, I questioned.

I felt discarded. I just didn't understand why he would dump me in the shelter to start another family, have another kid. Another kid who he was looking after. Why couldn't he do the same for me?

Eight

I WAS ALWAYS SO ANGRY and upset. And I moved back and forth between Siviwe and Ons Plek.

Every time I was moved to Siviwe, Lea stayed at Ons Plek. She was committed to staying safe. She hardly every left the shelter. The times I came back to see her she always seemed like she was doing better. I loved her; she was like a little sister. Our relationship faded when I moved to Siviwe, but I always remembered that she was there at Ons Plek, trying to stay safe.

While I was at Siviwe, I tried to stay clean, but sometimes it just got too much for me, and I would go back to the streets.

Occasionally I would go back to my mother in Khayelitsha. After a while, my circle of moving also landed me back at my dad's house.

Even after everything that had happened, I still felt good about seeing him – I would come and go maybe once a month. He'd let me know when Beverly wasn't there and I'd rock up. I just wanted a relationship, and it was important for me to spend time with him.

When she was around, he wasn't happy to see me, but I'd have fun with him when Beverly wasn't there. We'd eat soft white bread with lots of Rama margarine, Simba Mexican chilli chips and Oros orange squash. He was a fun person, quite cool. But my dad drank a lot after he was kicked out of Woodstock.

We also played a game, snakes and ladders – throw the dice and move your stone up or down. It was fun. Every time we ate together, we'd play that.

We didn't discuss problems. I didn't tell him that my mother didn't want me – he couldn't have known it would turn out the way it did. I never asked him for anything because we'd both lost a home and a family we loved.

Sometimes he would let me sleep overnight on the floor, but the next morning I would have to jump on the train back to town.

Sometimes I couldn't sleep over, and would have to leave at night. I took many train rides at night, travelling back to Ons Plek, or to under the bridge. Train rides at night meant I faced being molested by guys who would drag me to the toilets and do things to me.

One time as I was on the train from Gugs, on my way with some other girls from Ons Plek to town for a Brenda Fassie show. I somehow didn't feel fear when we were approached on the train by some aggressive men.

That night the train didn't stop at all the stations so we couldn't jump off. But it wasn't me who was raped that time.

And I just kept moving, on the streets, sometimes in the shelter, back and forth to my dad's house to flop on the floor for the night, then back to the streets. Always moving.

Because I was in and out of school all my childhood, I never attained enough education to move smoothly from one grade to the next; rather, I was always put in a special learner class for kids from the streets, like myself.

Eventually I ended up back in Siviwe, and after that I went to Batavia Secondary School, which was for special needs kids, because my reading levels and learning were low compared to other kids of my age. I settled down again, and tried to keep things steady.

Back in Gugs, my dad's shebeen business didn't do well, so Beverly went off to Joburg to deliver drugs. She got caught and was locked up, and that's the last I ever heard about her.

With no income, my dad couldn't pay his rent, so he went onto the streets to deal drugs. I don't know where his son, Storm, was taken.

After that, I saw my dad sometimes on the streets in Salt River, near Siviwe. He didn't always recognise me, but I still hung out with him before the Siviwe gates closed. Sometimes he would give me a R100 note, and I would brag about him to the other kids.

Every week the shelter gave us money to do our shopping at Shoprite, and we would sometimes see my dad on the streets begging. The other kids began to make fun of him, and this made me very angry.

The shelter had lots of girls who shared their beds: it was quite common among the shelter girls in order to secure a place in that society.

By now I had learnt only one way of dealing with my deep-seated feelings of hurt, batrayal and rejection: sex. I became this butch girl, and I took out my frustration on one of the girls at the shelter, a childhood friend. I found myself abusing her in the same way that I had been abused. She never seemed to complain about the way I treated her – she would get annoyed at me if I went quiet, if I didn't touch her and seemed to not care. Then she'd become confused and jealous. It seemed to satisfy my anger.

Nine

BY THE TIME I WAS close to my seventeenth birthday, I had become more focused. I knew that if I behaved well, I would be able to stay in the shelter for the year after I turned eighteen.

I went to school. I went to the tutoring sessions. I went to all the sessions with the shelter's volunteers and funder. I did all my duties. I didn't go out much. I was still with Freckles, but he was in jail again by then, and so even he wasn't a distraction – in fact, after that, I never saw him again.

In 1997, Michael Jackson arranged for the Ons Plek kids to see his show at Green Point Stadium.

It was an incredible night. We were so well behaved because we felt really important and respected. To get ready, we had done our hair, used all our hairclips, put on lip gloss and worn our most fashionable crop tops. We were very prepared because we thought we were going to meet Michael Jackson as we had uTata.

In the stadium, we were given great seats right at the front, and although we never met him it was a great night. When he sang 'I believe the children are our future', this spotlight lit up our row – and there were all these Cape Town street children. We were all so excited that Michael Jackson had seen us, and when he threw a kiss we all claimed it was aimed at us.

We really felt like he knew us. Ons Plek did have its benefits – it made some great memories for me.

One day, when I was at Siviwe, someone told me my dad had been found dead on the street. It was a terrible shock, and I had sudden fits of crying at the loss of another loved one; first my two great-grandparents, and now my dad. I was in standard 8 at Batavia Secondary School, but I left after that year because I felt so lost after my dad died.

I missed him so much.

My social worker and I thought that if I attended his funeral and met his mother and other relatives, that might be an opportunity for me to join their family. I thought it was a nice plan, because I remembered staying at my dad's mother's house on a farm way out of Cape Town when I was five years old.

She was called Auntie Em. I remembered quite a lot about my visit, even though I was so young. I had made friends with a white boy, Japie, the son of the white farmer. Japie was a boer boy with yellow hair. The water at the farm was salty, so we had to go to Japie's well for fresh water. And when we went to town, we had to take a donkey to the bus stop. There were a lot of beautiful tall trees and I'd had fun there, although I hadn't stayed long.

I was excited about meeting my dad's family, and that maybe I could go to live with them. But at the funeral, nobody knew who I was. Nobody even said hello. My social worker told my granny Em who I was, but she didn't recognise me, and she said she was too old to take care of more children.

I went back to the city even though I wanted to leave, to get out. It's amazing how your life can be happy and then go backwards again, and then again. From Michael Jackson nights to something like this.

One day, somebody came to me while I was sitting outside.

'Did you hear? Lea is dead.'

Apparently she had been walking on the mountainside at Lion's Head, which I found strange since she didn't like to leave the shelter. She came across a group of men. They raped her, and then stoned her to death.

I had lost yet another person.

I made plans to run out. I had to go to that spot to see for myself. I went looking for something; I wasn't sure what. The walk was long. When I got to the spot, I just sat and sat and sat. While I was sitting there, I was thinking of ways of getting out of the city. My dad, who hadn't want me, was gone; my best friend was gone ...

I thought: So, just go.

One thing about being at the shelter was that the gates were closed at 9pm. I sat there until 8pm. When I got back down the mountain, the gates were closed, and so instead I went to the bridge. I went there and smoked weed.

I just wanted to smoke as much as I could. I needed to.

Lea was somebody I could talk to. Her loss made me feel so emotional; her death upset and angered me so much that I didn't want to stay in the shelter any more. But at almost eighteen, I was experiencing an emotional breakdown.

After Lea died, I remained under the bridge for a whole week. I was thinking how I had to get out of this life in Cape Town; I had to find something better.

While I was there, I met this nice girl called Ntombi. She was an educated girl with a family, but she hung out with us under the bridge that week, smoking with us and telling stories.

Ntombi knew our ways, even though she had never had to enter our world. She brought us old clothes, and if she went to a party, she brought us the leftover food.

She was so nice to us. We hung out at the bridge together, and that's how Ntombi and I became friends. Ntombi told me she was going to Joburg, and I told her I was thinking of leaving too. I asked her for her number there, so we could stay in contact. I said I was going to call her the minute I was released from the shelter.

I kept that number as if it was the most important thing in the world to me, because while we were smoking she was describing this great life in Joburg. Everything about it sounded so amazing. And I thought that was what I wanted.

So one day I stood at the robot at the V&A Waterfront, close to the bridge where we'd been staying, and I gave two men blow jobs. That gave me enough money to pay for the train to Joburg.

I went back to the shelter, and I kept checking on my money, which I kept hidden in a takkie. After that I called her every now and again, to keep checking that she was expecting me.

Ten

I WAS A STREET SURVIVOR, having learnt how to steal, how to defend myself, how to find protection and how to fight off what I thought would harm me – survival instincts that had been developed in my system from the age of nine.

I didn't mind being smelly and dirty, or having ripped clothes. I lived with street people, and on the street I'd found people that I loved.

At eighteen, I decided to give up street life, and go to Johannesburg to find a job and a new life. I contacted Ntombi, who was a university student in Joburg.

Ntombi was sympathetic when I told her that I thought there were greener pastures in Joburg. She agreed to let me stay with her in Yeoville when I arrived, until I found my way.

Two days before I left Cape Town, I called her again and she said I should call when I arrived in Park Station. She was so excited for me, she said. For me, it was that feeling of having something so exciting to look forward to – my new life. Ntombi reassured me that everything was going to be great, that we'd hang out and do stuff together.

Everything in me was just so, so excited to be taking this step. Ntombi was in Joburg to study so I knew she had great connections. I couldn't wait to see her.

I had packed my stuff and I was ready. I had my bottle of glue, I had three zols, I had buttons wrapped up in paper. I had a pair of jeans and one tight top. I had this funny bomber jacket, roll-on deodorant, a face cloth and soap in a see-through plastic bag.

My train was leaving late afternoon. Third class.

But a whole lot was going to change.

A whole lot.

The train journey was thrilling, but long. And then I arrived at the busy station in Joburg. I was so excited as I called Ntombi on the payphone at the station. My eagerness and happiness at hearing her voice overwhelmed me. She said she would pick me up in two hours' time. While I waited I smoked some weed, and I got high as I sat there.

Two hours later, Ntombi appeared with a male friend, her hair straightened and her face made up, which made her look more mature than when I had last seen her under the bridge in Cape Town. Ntombi always had a happy face, and her big bum rounded out her short stature. She greeted me with a big hug, smelling of perfume.

Her friend drove us to a townhouse in Yeoville, where I thought she must be staying, and dropped us off.

As I walked in the front door, I was aware of the pleasant, fresh smell of the wooden floors. She showed me to a room. It was a very empty room and so I said to her, 'Wow, your room is so empty.'

And she said ja, but I mustn't worry because as we went through the year we'd buy stuff and fill it up. I took that at face value. Then she told me to rest a bit while she went out to get me some food, and she walked out the room.

The clean smell gave me a sense of safety. I'd had a lot to smoke and drink on the train, so I lay down and fell asleep on the floor. I slept for about three hours.

I never saw Ntombi again.

I was woken up by men hitting and punching me, removing my clothes and stripping me naked. Before I could figure out what was happening, masking tape was put around my eyes. I was punched and kicked because in my confusion I kept asking where Ntombi was.

Eventually they spoke, they said, 'Well, didn't your friend tell you?'

That's when my heart really leapt into my throat. It was the most indescribable shock. And so just lay there confused, in shock, and unable to move.

At first I thought they were going to kill me. Then I thought they were going to cut something from my body. I just didn't know what they were going to do.

Nothing could have prepared me for what came next. They

then tied me up and left. They were the first of many.

Why me, why me, why me.

That's what I kept on saying.

And then all the other painful memories of my life came flooding back.

Why me?

And then one guy came back and punched me in the stomach. When I tried to scream, he gave me ecstasy and gave me injections on my legs, my thighs. I could only hear that the people were getting quieter and quieter, and the city outside was getting quieter.

It must be night, I thought.

Later a guy came in. He had strong cologne on.

He told me that because I am new in Joburg, I must be fresh with no experience. He was happy to teach me, he said.

I let him know that I knew nothing.

By the time he was on top of me, I was already high, and hopeless.

My vagina kept going wet and dry. I heard this guy take spit out of his mouth with his hand; he slapped me complaining about what he now had to do. Then I held my breath.

I just held my breath, that's all I could do; I would close my eyes and try to lose consciousness. That would happen. And I would not breathe at all.

It went on for a couple of hours. And I don't know when he left.

Every day different men would come in and do what they wanted with me. I had no way of knowing who came in and who went out.

One guy wanted anal sex.

At that point, I thought I could almost see. It felt like the tape was coming off my eyes. He held my head back, he pulled really hard.

At times one guy would be doing his thing one side of my body while another guy did his thing on the other side, and then my mind would just switch off. And that would be it.

The guy eventually ejaculated, the one at the back.

I vomited because I had got used to the technique of holding my breath.

When they were done, they left.

I could smell my own vomit. I sat in the same position until the next day. They would come back in to refresh the drugs in my body. I was never given any food or anything to drink.

One guy said, 'You're such a bitch, you even dirtied the floor.'

My eyes were really burning and my mouth was dry.

My legs were numb.

My body got used to the drugs.

On the last day I was there, many men came through. Probably only about six. But the forth one was really crazy. He asked me to sit on top of him. And whenever he felt like it was good, he would burn my back with his cigarette.

And so I kept focusing on not moving faster, keeping a slow pace so he would stop pressing that cigarette in my back. He was crazy. He eventually ejaculated. Then gave me a sip of Jack Daniels and told me that it was the only way my cigarette wounds would heal.

And then he poured it over my back.

That last day went really slowly. Because I kept on counting my breaths. I could hear myself breathe when I didn't have clients. And suddenly a noise came through.

A younger girl was brought in and her screaming woke me up and made me worry, because it was the first time I had heard an outside person.

She screamed, 'What did I do wrong? What did I do wrong?'

I could hear by the sound of her voice how scared she was. How young. I could only hear her because my eyes were still taped shut. And it really scared me because I could hear that she had no idea what was happening. She had probably just been kidnapped. It was then that I realised I was being exchanged.

They opened a door and punched her and she cried again.

And then they grabbed me and threw me out the door.

After two weeks, I was swapped with this new girl, and I was thrown out of the house and onto the streets of Joburg in the middle of the night.

And that was it.

I smelt of sperm because my body had been soaked in it for two weeks. And I smelt of the Jack Daniels. And pee from wetting myself.

And once I was in the fresh air, I tried to smell Ntombi's perfume, hoping I would find her. I fell asleep.

But the first car sound woke me up.

And once again I was a street kid, waking up to car sounds.

Only this time it was in a city I didn't know.

Everything I had owned was gone – my bag, my clothes. Not that it mattered by then.

When they dumped me, I still had masking tape over my face. And I wasn't fully dressed. I was wearing these short little shorts and a lace top. Not my clothes.

From there I was on my own, left to survive on these Joburg

streets that I didn't know. Inside me, there was this huge anger at life, that I just hated life and what it had meant for me.

The only thing I wanted at that point were the drugs that would take my feelings away.

I needed clothes to cover myself and I went to look in the bins on the street. That's where I met this old Zulu begger.

In his drunken state, he saw I needed help. He helped me to remove the masking tape that was still stuck all over my face. When we pulled the tape from my eyes, it felt like my eyelids were being ripped off. I had angry red bruises around my eyes for a couple of months after that.

At the same time as the Zulu man was helping me, he was shouting at me in his broken street-isiZulu. It was like he was warning me: 'You young people don't listen, you just think about of the big city lights of Joburg but you don't know what can happen to you here ...' On and on, he shouted.

I felt love in that shouting because I felt he was caring for me, like a parent figure. I welcomed that. I asked him for clothes. He was wearing a maroon tracksuit top and boots. While he was shouting he took off his jacket and gave it to me.

I smelt his stink, his pee – and I knew I smelt as bad as him.

I went through a crying fit and he just let me cry.

Then we slowly we started to talk. He lived in one of the bins, he said. I learnt that he had come to Johannesburg ten years ago on a church outing from KwaZulu-Natal, but something had happened, somebody had cursed him, and he'd ended up on the streets. He swung his one gloved hand as he talked.

I needed to get money. I needed to get cleaned up and to get a fix. I knew I needed a guy who would give me money in exchange for pleasure.

So I left him and I walked to Park Station like this, in the Zulu man's jacket, to where the truck drivers park their trucks to rest. One thing about Joburg is that if you are wearing an oversized, torn jacket, nobody bothers with you. They think you're mad, so nobody touches you.

I had sex with a truck driver so I could buy clothes and dress myself.

And I smelt so bad that he then told me to take a shower. I used that money for the R5 shower and some for new clothes. Then I went back to the street in Yeoville to look for the old man, to return his jacket and give him R50 for helping me.

I was thinking like a street child again – surviving like I had survived in Cape Town. And that's one thing the street teaches: older street people protect us, and so we younger ones must respect our elders. There is an understanding. The elders allow us to sleep in their boxes if we're robbed; that's how they keep us safe. If we steal from a Kentucky Fried Chicken outlet and have lots of chicken, and we put it in an elder's trolley for safekeeping, he won't take anything unless we offer him some. Even if we hide a five-litre boxed wine in their stuff, the old people won't touch it.

So I was paying my dues.

Another reason I wanted to find my old man was because he knew Johannesburg – Yeoville, Hillbrow, Berea – and I thought he could help me around. Playing innocent, I told him I wanted to visit the clubs 'for a husband'.

But really, at that point my only thought was how I could get money for drugs.

That night, my Zulu friend and I walked to Berea so that he could show me the clubs. We walked silently and slowly as I regained my strength. He showed me the clubs on Bree Street, where he left me, saying, '*Uzothola amadoda laphaya*'. And so I walked into what would be my life from then on.

I have had people ask me why I didn't go straight to the police that night after my trafficking. I answer that I didn't think anyone would listen to me.

By then I knew my friend Ntombi had been paid to get me into that house. The money that she made selling me had probably paid for her to study at university. My dreams had fed her dreams.

And I had really thought she was a friend.

After that, how could I trust anybody?

And also, the police had never protected me in Cape Town. We street kids had always been told that we 'liked' the things they did to us in the jail cells. But mostly, I think, it was because my body was drugged up. And that's what it all was about after that.

Drugs.

Eleven

AFTER MY RELEASE FROM THE house, the first thing I craved was drugs. I became a prostitute from the age of eighteen, because I needed money for drugs.

All the prostitution I did on Joburg's streets was always for money and drugs. There was nothing other than that, no money to get out.

And there was so much anger. Your day looks like night, your night looks like day. And everywhere you look are the reflections of what has happened to you.

In the days after my violent trafficking ordeal, as I made my way on the streets in Johannesburg, I met Margaret and the Hillbrow girls.

I was so numb. But I needed to feel numb. I needed to earn money to buy the drugs that made me numb. I was so desperate for those drugs to take me away from my thoughts. When I wasn't high on drugs, I was shy, insecure and afraid.

The first time I met Margaret, it was obvious to her that I was very new.

Margaret was from Durban, a Zulu woman, and she was tough but welcoming. She could also be quiet and kind, and she told me straight out to be nice to her and the other girls.

'We're not here to hurt each other,' she told me, referring to the street girls, 'but this is how it works.'

She knew what we needed to do to survive on the streets and she could come on quite strong. She'd reassure us girls by saying, 'We're OK doing this.'

And that's how I entered prostitution; to escape from my situation.

I knew I needed to 'learn the ropes', learn how things worked and who was who in the business. She proceeded to mentor me in the ways of prostitution so that I too could make some money. The prostitution we did also involved how to get drugs for yourself, and how to push drugs to your clients.

'We're going to teach you,' she said.

I never told Margaret or the other girls about my experience coming to Joburg.

I just told her, 'Teach me.'

Margaret was able to get me a temporary place to stay with the other Hillbrow girls. As I built my relationship with her, I knew I had to be careful not to fall into her hands, and be pimped by her. I tried hard to keep my independence. Even though I relied on her.

She gave me some of her clients, which at first I found scary in my newness to it all, but the clients were gentle with me.

Once, she discounted a client so that I could do him favours in the car while she taught me a good technique for giving blow jobs – it was a crazy way of doing things, but also a way for us girls to care for and learn from each other. And that's how I learnt to keep a condom in my mouth, skilfully put it on the top side of my tongue and rolling it back and forth, which is how I avoided the client's fluids from coming into contact with my mouth tissue.

Years later, due to rot and infection, I had to get a back molar removed by a dentist. I faked pain in the other back molar and asked for it to be removed as well purely so that I had more space available for the condom I used to hide in the back of my mouth during blow jobs.

The first money I earned Margaret took from me, but I didn't worry about that as I was still learning.

The Hillbrow girls would come back to the house where we lived at around four or five in the morning. They'd sit around and smoke, count their money, and discuss whether they'd had a good night. For the first little while I just sat around with them and listened to them describing their sexual episodes. But as I hung around the girls, I started to get more and more clients.

And bought more drugs.

I have since been back to Hillbrow to look for Margaret and the girls. I couldn't find them. The area has changed, the buildings are more run down, but prostitution continues.

I was with Margaret for my first three months in Joburg. She was like a big sister to me. At that time, in the late nineties, we black girls didn't get the same chance to work in night clubs as the white girls did, which is why we often had to work on the streets. The Nigerian pimps knew this, and they gave us a hard time.

Pimps make their money by selling girls and drugs to clients. A pimp could just use me as he wanted and then give me R100. Or for the whole night, I might get R300, while the pimp makes loads of cash from selling 'his' girls and drugs – enough cash to buy a car.

Then he'd ride around in his big car checking up on us.

The pimps had a lot of power because they also sold drugs to us girls, and that's how we became dependent on them. What a girl gets out of the partnership is accommodation, a fake 'boyfriend' – who lies, manipulates and emotionally blackmails her – and maybe three meals a day. She also gets a drug addiction. The minute the pimp buys her a drink in the club, he has already dropped a drug in her drink, and that's how it starts.

You risked violence from a pimp if you owed him money, but it was hard to avoid. When you're dependent on the pimp's drugs, you are trapped.

Sometimes I couldn't pay a pimp for my drugs. He would give me clients in exchange, until I'd paid him back, and during those times I wouldn't even have money for my toiletries – it all went to the pimp for my drugs. To get out of this situation, I would have to play my cards right – work for this pimp for the next three weeks, get high, and also secure some clients for future work. Then leave, with no cash.

Sometimes a pimp would sell me off to a client.

In those early days, while I was in Hillbrow, a pimp I was working for gave me over to three guys who had just come out of jail.

It was winter time, cold, and drugs were hard to come by. At that time I was dependent on a pimp whose typical clients were gangster types from Soweto. I owed the pimp money for drugs so these gangsters paid the pimp directly and I was never paid.

I was sold, a sex slave, to these gangsters.

I was locked up in a building and I was raped and physically abused for three days, forced to do anything they said in order to avoid them punching and kicking me. During that terrible time, the only thing I could do to find any relief was smoke weed – trying desperately to get away, to a place beyond my body.

It's hard to describe the violence, but the closest explanation I can now come up with would be sadism, the enjoyment they got from abusing another person.

Being trafficked to these gangsters for these three days was no different to the two weeks I had suffered when I first arrived in Joburg. Once the pimp had retrieved the money I owed him, he let me go.

Afterwards, I probably didn't look like someone who had been gang raped. I looked like a drug addict. I was dirty, smelly and I hadn't bathed.

Traumatised, I went to the clinic and told the nurse, 'I was just raped by a lot of men. I just want some help and if you can clean out my wounds.'

The nurse said to me, 'You think this is Shoprite? You come here to get your stuff clean and then go back to what you were doing? We're not here to clean you so that you go back and do the same thing again! We're here to clean you so you don't go back again!'

I just looked at her and felt like punching her because she had no idea what I had just come from. Or how I had got to be here.

I had no money.

All I wanted was for her to clean me.

She refused to help me and so I left. Instead, I went to the Zimbabwean and Zulu girls, who knew traditional medicine. They told me to take TimJan, which I could buy from the chemist. It is a strong, bitter health juice with a vinegar taste. They told me to drink that, and also lots of hot water.

You drink half a cup of TimJan with lots of water through the night and through the next day, and it cleans out the body. It burns badly in the stomach and is supposed to be drunk in small amounts. But after the things that happened to us in Hillbrow, we would drink the whole bottle. I always hoped, back then, that I would be OK. After what happened to me that time, the girls also told me I should clean out my vagina with Jeyes Fluid.

There were times when we had wars with the Nigerian pimps. It could happen when the girls stuck together. The Zulu and Zimbabwean girls I knew mostly didn't take drugs so that's why they could beat up the pimps, to prove what strong hustlers they were. The girls even carried knives. If a girl got robbed by a pimp, the other girls formed a team to chase and catch him.

The Nigerian pimps had drugs to sell to the white clients, but we black girls wanted the white clients to pay better for sex – and we were OK dealing directly with clients.

So that's also how war might start. After we had got to

know a client through a pimp, we would beat up the pimp so he wouldn't come back to our corner. We would sometimes send out a new girl to entice him to our spot, and then beat him up when he followed her. That's how we made sure he would stay away.

We also made friends with the drag queens. The drag queens had boyfriends who were gangsters, and the gangsters would fight the tsotsis to protect us. A gangster would come in a '*gusheshe*', a BMW, with an electric roof and big tyres, and beat up anyone molesting us. So that's how we girl gangs – the Zulu and Zim and Xhosa girls – owned those streets. Without those roaming pimps, we could sometimes take over the streets of Hillbrow.

But we were never safe.

I would sometimes get to a point when the more high I could get on drugs, the more clients I could handle. Then the realisation would hit: 'Hey, I can do this on my own! I don't need no pimp.'

But if you show that kind of arrogance, you get slapped. If you cross the line with a pimp, anything can happen.

Death lived just around the corner.

There was a way I could get off the streets: if a client liked me enough, he could buy me off my pimp. If a client paid R4000, then the pimp would release me. There were always other girls for him to exploit.

The client would then introduce me to a club that he attended regularly. I could start working there, and he would become my regular client. He could then give me a good reference: he could tell others that I'm great, I'm healthy, I'm not a junky and don't use drugs too much, that I have incredible energy, that I don't fight. These clients could introduce me to bigger and better clients. Girls brag about these opportunities.

But of course, I wouldn't be any part of the conversation with the pimp. I never had the power to make my own decisions. After the arrangements were made, both the pimp and the client would tell me what a big favour they were doing me by getting me off the streets.

But even if I was working off the streets, it didn't mean I was safe. Clients could be as brutal and abusive as pimps, and anything could happen to me when I got into a client's car.

I was always on my own, always at risk.

Twelve

THE MOST PAINFUL PARTS OF that life were having to experience rapes and sexual intercourse with forced penetration. After these events, I would go to the chemist and get the morning-after pill. Even more than the sex acts themselves, I was angry that I had to try to suck out this stuff that men put into my body.

I soon learnt on the streets that my health had to be taken care of as this career was my money and my survival. I had to look after myself. So, after buying my drugs, I spent most of the rest of my money on health-related maintenance – home remedies, medicines and doctor visits – because the more sex there was, the more doctor's appointments I needed.

When we needed to, we would collect R500 as a group, and go to the doctor and tell him to clean us. Some Zulu doctors would spray our bums with disinfectant. Or we would buy a special plastic tube with gel which we used for cleaning out the vagina.

Men paid a lot for anal sex; I don't know why. It was very painful for me. I hated this aspect of satisfying my client, and I always had to go to the doctor afterwards because I would bleed a lot. Mostly, I hated this position because of the way it was done to me: it always felt like rape, and it brought back too many painful memories.

There were other things we street girls learnt to do to look after our health. During my menstrual periods, I used a sponge – just the kind of sponge we use to wash dishes – covered with strong soap to soak up the blood during and after sex. I didn't like using tampons because they got in the way of my work. I had to be ready at all times, and take all the work I could get – a period was not a good enough reason not to take a client.

After a shift with a client, the sponge would get stuck way up in the vagina. In the morning, I would go to the bath and sit on a bucket of hot steaming water and let the steam go up into the vagina to be absorbed by the sponge so that it gradually oozed its way out of the cavity.

Getting the sponge out was a time when my emotions would kick in, because it really hurt to get it out. The frustrations of the job, and all the hassles – those were the things I would be thinking about as I took this time to sit on a bucket. I always felt anxious doing this, so I would have to calm myself down with a cigarette in my hand, and a zol, trying to straighten out my confused mind.

The sponge was a good thing, but using it could also turn into a bad experience. In my time, I saw some girls who couldn't get the sponge out. They would smell rotten for days. You needed good friends who cared about you to help you at times like this. But sometimes it was unavoidable, and you could miss out on clients because of this issue when there's nobody around to help you get the sponge out. We bought braai tongs to use when the sponge got stuck, and that was unpleasant.

We took the morning-after pill to prevent getting pregnant. I only knew my fertile time was 'before and after' my periods, and had been told by the shelter mothers in my teens that the bleeding was the result of 'old eggs breaking'.

I had to be careful I didn't go back to the same chemist for the morning-after pill, because some chemists would ask for my details. So we girls had to go to different chemists to avoid being discovered as prostitutes. A client might even have to drive me around looking for different chemists!

In the case of a rape, I would immediately go to the clinic and ask the nurse to help clean me up. Some nurses would wait before asking my name, and want to take a report first. I would say, 'Voetsek. Just clean me up.'

Some nurses, knowing we girls lived on the streets, made it difficult for us to get the medical assistance we needed. We felt that we were just vulnerable girls being subjected to open abuse in society – so sometimes, as a group, we girls would go to the clinic and mess it up to teach them a lesson.

So, after drugs, health was always at the top of the minds of us street girls. If I had any money left over after drugs and medicine, it was used for clothes.

I was now nineteen years old, and had spent some time being

pimped on the streets in central Johannesburg. I decided that I wanted to do prostitution by myself, off the streets, and away from the manipulative pimps who had so much power over me.

I needed new clients and I wanted a place where there weren't a lot of other prostitutes, as there were in Hillbrow and Berea. I asked around for some help, and a friend, one of the girls I knew from Hillbrow, led me to Steve in Benoni.

Steve managed the Benoni fire station and ran the training programme for firemen there. My friend knew the girls who visited their firemen boyfriends at the fire station. I was introduced to Steve because I needed a place to stay. Always wearing his blue overalls, Steve welcomed me, with his square Indian face, with eyes that carefully met my own gaze. He allowed me to sleep at the fire station in return for having sex with him.

Unlike the other girls, I didn't want a fireman boyfriend and I wasn't just out to have fun with the guys. I wanted clients so I could earn money for my drug habit. And that is how I started working in the clubs of Benoni: when the firemen's girlfriends went to hang out at the clubs, I hung out with them, making my money privately so that I wouldn't embarrass them. On weekends, if I wasn't working, I would just find a place at the fire station to put my head and sleep. Unlike the other girls, I wasn't there to party.

Benoni was a quiet place, and the fire station was not far from the few night clubs and the mall. We girls would go to one club, Planet Cats, which was near the Benoni lake. It was a cool place, with great DJs who were just starting out.

At Planet Cats, the boys would watch while the girl groupies danced and flirted. I was the one who went to a specific corner, in the back, to play around with a guy who would pay me R150 or R200.

I wasn't really strict on the price at that point; at nineteen, that was a lot of money for me. I took whatever I could get.

You learn to avoid street problems by hanging out in clubs. You learn that a club is a place to chill out, and you don't leave until you have a client. That's how you roll.

I'd buy my first drink, making sure it was a strong one, and then I'd take my time with it until someone bought me my next drink. Because I'd be thinking to myself, 'You ain't got no money, girl, to spend on your own drinks!'

My cigarettes saved me. A cigarette is a good way to connect with a person. There's always somebody smoking. I'd think to myself, 'I don't have to carry any lighter because I'm a woman! Some guy will light it.' And this worked because that's how I would start chatting to someone. That's how the conversation would kick in.

Then I'd get drunk or high, and get taken out by a client. I usually wouldn't know where I was going or what I'd find there. As the client and I walked out together, the bouncer would sometimes tell the clients to use a condom, but the guy would normally just wave it off.

So that's how I met my clients.

And I thought Benoni was good to me. It was a quiet neighbourhood, mostly Afrikaans, with no prostitutes on the streets. I could get clients, and I could work in the clubs. I didn't have to stand on the streets, or deal with rip-off pimps.

A friend of Steve's saw that I didn't have a proper home, and that I was just living at the fire station. He suggested that I come to work at his bar.

NgiloNgilo was a nice place in Benoni, an African jazz bar named after an African struggle song; people who were into jazz and poetry went there. It was next to a big funeral parlour company.

Sisi Chuma owned and ran the bar. She was tall and wore Xhosa dreadlocks. She was a woman who talked tough. Her skin was oiled to make it look shiny.

I worked as a waitress there and was given permission to sleep in the storeroom at night, so I left the fire station.

The problem was that I had to be in my room by 10pm since the storeroom was locked overnight. That meant I couldn't run out and get my drugs when I needed them, and I only had weed to smoke during the week. I started sipping on bottles of alcohol from the storeroom, taking care that none of the bottles got empty so quickly that Sisi Chuma would notice.

That was also the trade-off about Benoni: it was a nice place, but it also wasn't easy getting drugs there, so I had to take the train to Kempton Park in my off hours.

Sunday was my only off day, so I organised it that on a Saturday night I'd serve at the bar and then find a client to leave with so that it appeared to Sisi Chuma that he was my boyfriend. I couldn't do this on a regular basis though, because Sisi Chuma would notice.

'Oh, you have so many boyfriends on the weekends!' Sisi Chuma would smirk at me, with one front tooth shining brown and grey.

I had three guys who were regular clients at the bar, and who liked the idea that I was selling sex. I saw them on weekends, when I could also meet their friends and make deals. One of the regulars tried to pimp me by acting like my boyfriend – he didn't know that I already knew how things worked. He'd drop me off at his friend's place for favours and selling drugs. This was all done quietly, because I still needed to keep things secret from Sisi Chuma.

Although I found that a bit upsetting, things seemed to be going fine. I had a real job working at the bar as well as my clients, so I was getting double pay. I enjoyed free alcohol because guys at the bar would buy me drinks, although I didn't drink if I was already high on weed.

On Sundays, I could travel to Kempton Park for my drugs and get very high, and I'd still have enough weed to smoke during the week. I picked my drugs according to my needs: there were drugs for weekdays, drugs for boring days, drugs for fun days, drugs for the weekends.

I thought I had balance in my life.

Thirteen

I worked at NgiloNgilo until I got pregnant.

I was twenty years old, and it came as a shock.

I hadn't used condoms during any of my exploits. Trying to prepare for sex by taking condoms with me to work, giving them to clients or trying to use them in the middle of a session simply didn't work. When I was with a client, I was too busy trying to earn my money, and the guys were too busy trying to get their groove on. I also never had any contraceptive injections, and we girls didn't know about the woman's condom. While the condom was important for preventing infection in the mouth, I rarely used one for vaginal penetration. But this did not occur much anyway since clients preferred other positions.

It was the combination of alcohol and drugs that made the decision, and pregnancy was not on my mind.

So I was surprised by my pregnancy, and it frustrated me.

It interfered with my job security and my living arrangements. I had got used to this routine of mine.

The father of my baby was a client, but a loving one. I thought I maybe saw a relationship developing between us, and he didn't think I was a prostitute because he didn't know about my other clients.

When I told the father of my baby about my pregnancy, he ran away and I never saw him again.

Hilmanton was Shona-speaking, and he became attracted to me because I was pregnant. He used the expression, '*Ukuthandwa kwesisu*' (the symptoms of pregnancy make you attractive to men).

To men like Hilmanton, pregnancy is very beautiful, indicating that a woman is fertile and can have children. What it didn't mean was that he wanted *this* child; he didn't want people to think *he* had made me pregnant with this baby I was carrying.

'If you have an abortion, I'll marry you,' he tried to convince me.

Hilmanton would pick me up in his nice BMW and drive us to a bar to chat. We had a lot of sex in his car. It was all an adventure for him. He was tall, dark, handsome and very well educated.

And he felt sorry for me.

I knew I was developing feelings for him. I was comfortable

with him; he treated me nicely. I thought he was worth it.

We looked everywhere for a clinic to perform the abortion.

Hilmanton wanted to do everything legally so there would be no mess-up. But the clinics refused because I was too far along with the pregnancy.

So Hilmanton left, he disappeared and never came back.

For several months I tried to hide my pregnancy from Sisi Chuma.

One day, she asked me straight out, 'What are you going to do with the baby? I can't keep you here like this.'

Since abortion was by now out of the question, Sisi Chuma eventually decided to let me stay and work at the bar until I delivered the baby. She then offered to help me and suggested that I give the baby up for adoption. She arranged for me to go to an organisation in Parktown that provided a shelter for abandoned babies or babies being given up for adoption.

It was a nice place. Their house policy was that I had to write a letter to the baby, who would receive it at the age of eighteen, and I did that.

I was angry, hurt and confused, but I decided that with my way of life, I couldn't keep a baby.

I delivered my baby boy on 14 December 2001, seven days after my twenty-first birthday. I only saw his tiny face for a split second, right after his birth, before he was whisked away.

He was adopted immediately.

I named him Z.

After that, I got my job back with Sisi Chuma, and lived in the bar's storeroom again for a while. But Sisi Chuma and I weren't getting along, and I was afraid of meeting my baby's father at the bar, which would have been very painful for me.

Eventually, I stopped working at NgiloNgilo because every-one there was asking me where my baby was.

I felt the walls were caving in on me.

When I left NgiloNgilo, I was still hurt from having what I had thought was a caring man walk out on me because I couldn't have an abortion. It had also been very painful trying to get over the fact that I had given up my baby son.

I needed to find myself again. I needed time to heal.

And I needed my own place to stay.

I met someone in a Benoni tavern, a man called Madoda. For R300 a month, his chubby aunt, Sisi Jabu, rented me a back room in their big house, which she ran like a guest house.

Sisi Jabu was a Zulu lady. She would gamble at the street corner, playing cards, smoking and sniffing tobacco with the men folk. She was very kind to me, and I grew very close to her family.

I paid up front for three months of rent and when I first arrived I wasn't looking for sex work.

Madoda had a crush on me. I was only twenty-one, and he was much older. He took the time to help me fix up my room, putting up black cotton fabric to cover the ceiling. Then we painted the walls orange! I wanted the room to be a dark place where I could smoke my weed and feel safe.

I had a single bed and a small table. Outside my room, there were rabbits in the garden, breeding like crazy. While I was smoking weed, I would just watch the rabbits bonking and laugh my head off – unlike so many clients I had met, the rabbits clearly didn't need Viagra! I had not had a pet since my cat, Ginger, back in Woodstock, and they reminded me of my life and childhood home, which now seemed so long ago. So I would go out to buy them cabbage and feed them. I really loved those rabbits.

At Sisi Jabu's place, I learnt how to live with a Zulu family. I learnt how to make this *amagayo* porridge, which was really nice, and I started getting comfortable in the kitchen. Every morning I would make a pot of porridge for everyone, and I got to know the other people in the house. There was a church lady, and a man who collected greyhounds. He trained them to run and race at the Benoni lake, and was always travelling to Durban, making big money.

The house felt to me like a real family environment. This Zulu family did everything together, and I found everyone very accommodating. I learnt isiZulu through speaking with the family, and I enjoyed their culture.

There was also no pressure on me: I didn't need to talk about my family, and they never asked about my past. Because they saw me smoking weed, they just thought I was this quiet Rastafarian girl. They didn't mind me smoking. I think they liked me – I made their house come alive.

As time passed, I started to need money, and so I started working again. If I had clients, I would mostly go to their place, but there were a few special clients who liked my small, hidden, quiet place, and I let them come to my room at Sisi Jabu's. Those clients would knock on my door at one in the morning, do their thing with me, then leave.

I just told Sisi Jabu they were my boyfriends. No one minded.

Madoda had a girlfriend in KwaZulu-Natal, and one time he brought her to visit. Unlike everyone else in the house, this woman wouldn't greet me. She stayed for two days.

A week later, I was infested with pig fleas in my arm pits,

my private parts and on my head. I was itching all over, crying in pain, and I was smoking more and more weed in order to tolerate the discomfort. I was in agony.

'You got cursed,' Sisi Jabu said. Somebody had put something at my door, she told me.

Sisi Jabu took me to a traditional healer, who gave me a ten-litre bucket full of an awful liquid made with herbal leaves. I had to bath in it and also drink it and vomit it up. I had never believed in these healers before, but this treatment worked: the fleas disappeared the next day.

'What caused this?' I asked Sisi Jabu, mystified.

'You were probably given this muti by Madoda's girlfriend. She was jealous of you.'

What horror I had gone through! Madoda and I had never had any kind of relationship – sexual or otherwise!

I didn't like this thing that had happened to me – it really shocked me. I was also angry with myself, as I had promised myself years before that I would never get close to anyone. From my first experience of sexual violence at the age of nine, I had trained myself to rely on people only for money and drugs. Other than that, I just didn't trust people. Period.

But now I had got close to this family of Sisi Jabu's.

I was physically exhausted from the sangoma's work on me. Now I had to deal with the fact that I had been cursed while staying with this family, and so soon after the pain of losing my baby son.

These disappointments finished me.

I had to find my escape.

I decided at this point that I would stay in the house, but that I needed to create a daily routine away from this Zulu family I had come to love and adore. I had got too comfortable with this family arrangement.

I needed more clients.

People have different ways of escaping. While living at Sisi Jabu's in Benoni, I started working as a waitress at the Circus Roadhouse restaurant in Boksburg. Opposite the roadhouse was a club, which had pool tables to hide the fact that there were rooms upstairs for having sex with the girls. Clients from the escort club used to come to the roadhouse to eat.

I met a white guy there one day and we started chatting. He asked me to leave the roadhouse with him. I wondered what an older white guy was wanting with a young black girl like me. We negotiated my fee and what he wanted to do with me, and then I went with him to his car.

As soon as we got in, he rolled up the car windows and started slapping me in the face.

'I'm about to rape you,' he said as he punched me.

And he did.

This is not what we had negotiated, but I knew I needed to treat him carefully. I couldn't fight back.

Then suddenly he said to me, 'I like this – it's like a fantasy. Please can we do this on a regular basis? I'll pay you.'

I thought, *Wow. OK. If this guy is going to pay me, then …*

'No problem,' I said.

He asked me how much I wanted.

'A thousand?' I answered.

'No problem.'

So after that we met up regularly after my shifts at the roadhouse. We would make arrangements to meet in his car, or in the bush, or at his house. Or we'd drive to a motel, and he'd make me act things out there. I'd wear young girls' clothes, and he'd make me do strange rape scenes – funny ones, crazy ones, all sorts.

Is this the kind of thing that happens to girls like me?

Yes. You can tell your potential client how much you charge and you can negotiate your terms, but that doesn't necessarily mean that things will happen the way you have agreed. And some people have strange, sordid needs. This is part of the cycle of repeated abuse.

Should I have resisted the violence done to my body?

I felt that if I was being paid, I should put up with the abuse. I did not have much self-esteem at that point in my life, and I didn't feel that I deserved better. And so I only resisted the violence when I was acting as a character in one of this guy's crazy scenes, not in reality.

Then the guy disappeared for a while. I started calling him on his home phone since the money had been good – R1000 every weekend. I also had bad bruises and wounds from him, which I knew he needed to take care of for me.

I started to threaten him, saying I knew where he lived. He finally came back and gave me some money.

He would have carried on, I think. But in the end I got tired of him.

Looking back at my younger years, I think I always wanted a real friend, and a nice partner to fall in love with. I wanted to have kids and find a good job. It's always been in the back of my mind.

But here I was in this life where I was paid to connect with people, to satisfy their needs but not my own. And it was all driven by this desperate addiction to drugs – the addiction that kept the cycle going, and which took away all my confidence as a person. The drugs took away my dreams for a better life.

Every now and again there would be a client who didn't want sex, but who just wanted to talk with me. I eventually became weary of this, though, wondering what his real intention was – because in all the time I did this work, I never found a client who really wanted to be my friend. Even the gentle guys.

And there were gentle clients. Clients who were having sexual difficulties with their partners, clients who just wanted to talk or cuddle. When I was very high on drugs or weed after a sexual encounter, I would enjoy a client's gentle words. Words like: 'You're so beautiful. You make me so happy, so comfortable ...'

Pillow talk.

But if I ever told a guy what *I* wanted, what *I* was feeling, he wouldn't answer.

There'd always be some sort of emotional tension with my regular clients – tension because at the back of my mind a voice would be saying, 'Don't become his friend.' Yet I also didn't want to lose them.

These are the contradictions that emerge from this lifestyle, because even with the drugs in my veins, I was still a woman with a beating heart.

Even if I was heartbroken.

Did I learn anything along the way? I never really *felt* anything: I just wanted my drugs. I lived in desperation for them. And even being prostituted seemed an escape from the overwhelming feelings of neglect, abandonment and disappointment that had tainted my young life.

Fourteen

ONE NIGHT, I WALKED FROM Sisi Jabu's place to a small Chinese shopping centre near the Eastgate mall, where there were a few clubs. I went to one and just hung around.

I waited for a while. At around ten, I got my first client. A guy invited me to have dinner with him.

Du-uh, I thought, *I need drugs, not food!*

Instead, I asked him if he had any cocaine.

Up until then, I had mostly been smoking weed and buttons. Button is mandrax – I just knew it was an acidic mixture of stuff taken from government hospitals. In my experience, among other things, it drains nutrients out of your skin. I used to drink a lot of water and used soap on my face to counteract the effects buttons had on the skin, but it wasn't a comfortable experience.

It was time for a change in drugs.

My client told me he didn't use coke, but said he could organise some for me. For now, he could only offer me a smoke and dinner.

At around midnight, he could see I was bored and needed a fix. He drove us towards Midrand, to a striptease club/escort house where Nigerian pimps and their girls sold drugs. I told him the coke would cost R300, which he gave me.

Inside, I breathed in the familiar smokey club smells. I was craving and I must have looked quite desperate. It didn't take me long to spot a girl I knew. I had met her a few times when I'd gone to Soweto. Her name was Ayanda, and she helped me get the drugs.

A man sold me two grams of coke for only R100, discounted because he said I must come back – I guess to be pimped by him. Not caring, I thanked him and went back to my client in the car. I happily stashed the extra R200 in my bra.

Back in the car, I took one snort of the coke and I immediately went crazy. I went straight for the guy's balls and gave him a blow job. I was feeling so good, sizzling. I buzzed, doing what I did best.

In the years to come, that became my package: coke plus sex. One without the other just didn't work.

'Are you hungry?' he asked me later.

I told him I was finished for the night. He didn't want to leave me, and told me he wanted me as his regular girl. He gave me R500 for a taxi home and to pay my rent.

Having a 'regular' boyfriend as a client was not my business. Nevertheless, we kept meeting at the club for a while.

I was still living at Sisi Jabu's house, but now I was more out than in. I was spending a lot of time in clubs, and I had started thinking about the world of stripping.

I knew that training as a stripper would be a bonus for my profession: moving up to working in the safety of a strip club is a major goal for any prostitute. It offered better income opportunities and was a way of avoiding the abusiveness of street pimps. Over the next few years I would come to learn that it had its own dangers, but at the time I thought it was a good option for me.

Near the shopping centre in Eastgate , a new strip club had just opened. I had been meeting this white guy about every other night at the reggae/hip hop nightclub downstairs and I was getting what I needed – drugs and clients. I was familiar with the place so I thought why not join this new strip club. It was a classy club, part of a chain that had branches in other towns in South Africa.

I didn't know how to strip, but when I went to talk to the club management they said they would train me on condition that I lost weight.

At the club there were skinny girls, fat girls, older girls and younger girls, but mostly white girls for a crowd of mostly white men. From the outside, the club was advertised just as a 'strip dance' club, but inside there were various rooms for various activities. The cigar bar would attract the rich businessmen and foreigners, who paid up front, and they would get certain girls the whole night.

I had been going back regularly to the Midrand club for my

coke, and had been seeing my good friend Ayanda, as she was still working there. Ayanda was shy and quiet and liked tagging along with me, and I wanted a girl around as a friend. I told Ayanda that she should join me and stay in my room at Sisi Jabu's house, and work as a stripper. She agreed.

The drama came when her pimp caught up with her for leaving the club. He would find her in Eastgate and beat her up, and she would have to come to my room during the day to fix her wounds. This went on for three weeks until the pimp found out that Ayanda was working for white people. Nigerians couldn't tackle whites at that time – it was too risky.

Now I had a steady job and was learning to strip, and I had my own clients and was getting my stash of drugs. And after that drama with the pimp, things started going well for Ayanda and me.

There were professional strippers from Asia and Russia at the strip club, as well as Afrikaans girls. Ayanda and I were the only black girls there, lifting our legs and jumping up and down on the poles with the other strippers.

And I was proud of my African body – it looked good, and my boobs were a real double-D. Those of the German girls were big and fake – they used silicon to enhance their breasts. The guys would take their brandy shots off my body, laughing and applauding Ayanda and me: 'Hey, these black chicks are real!'

I felt like an African lion queen! Money started to just fall around me. My first few months at the club were great.

This was now 2002, and I was feeling encouraged.

I had designed a candle-wax strip show, and I was becoming more creative with my work as a stripper. In the show, Ayanda would take two lit candles and drizzle the hot wax on my body as I writhed about, allowing it to pour onto my spread legs and private parts. I started improving my moves as well as my lingerie by wearing new G-string panties, which I bought with my extra earnings.

With my upgraded lingerie and suggestive movements, I was becoming a better and better stripper and dancer. Clients who knew the club and my work started hiring me for outside events, and I began to travel from town to town doing my act. Ministers – both of government and of the church – organised private parties and invited us strippers to attend, and I began visiting more places around South Africa. And as we visited other clubs, we learnt new techniques and innovative ways to strip.

Also, more black girls were starting in the profession, and the more black girls that started stripping, the more we challenged the international white girls who were also performing at these small clubs.

With lots of baby oil on our skin, we black girls glittered and shone like stars, and people loved it. We didn't copy the old moves either – we weren't going to just climb those poles. Rather, we became creative on the floor, inventing new moves and techniques.

The guys howled.

For our own safety and the success of the strip club's business, there were rules and regulations we had to follow. In the club, we only dealt with clients on the floor, and weren't supposed to sleep with them – otherwise, the authorities would come in and close the place down for being an illegal brothel. We had our own arrangements though, and we slept with clients anyway. So while not all of the girls could strip, all were engaged in sex because some clients would pay to see a girl in private. Also, we were not supposed to mix with clients after hours, because then they wouldn't come back to the club and support it.

The club also had ways of dealing with the drugs we were taking. The heart always races when on drugs – when a girl takes a bunch of ecstasy tablets, and half a bottle of Jack Daniels, the heart will be racing. So the club had a cold room with a box of ice where we'd be forced to go to cool down if we overdosed. This helped avoid heart attacks.

Between midnight and two in the morning, if your boss liked you and gave you the space, you could make around R8000 a night in the lap dance rooms. A client could touch me in these rooms, whereas on the strip floor touching was not allowed – he just had to pay for it. Clients paid R200 for fifteen minutes, R280 for half an hour, and R360 for an hour in these rooms for touching only, with club management occasionally peeping in to make sure all was in order. Of the R360 hourly rate, I would receive R120, and I was paid every night in cash.

In the lap dance rooms, when it was just us, I could slither my body against the client's body, give him what he wanted, and get extra payment. If a client wanted a blow job, the cash would be an extra payment for me alone.

For organising all-night bachelor parties outside, the club received R1500, of which half went to me and included an escort. The lap dance money covered my security escort to and from my residence, and my first three drinks of the evening.

As long as the money was good and the clients came and enjoyed what we were doing, everything was fine. I was making good money, so I didn't want problems or to get kicked out. I kept a clean slate. My good health meant being disciplined about my drug use. And I felt that I was safe: I even had a bodyguard to escort me by car to and from my accommodation at Sisi Jabu's. The hours were fine – our nights ended around seven in the morning, and we had the rest of the day to sleep and prepare.

I also didn't have to rely on outside clients for extra cash any more – I could earn more cash to pay for my drugs by servicing a client in the club's lap dance rooms.

With the money I was earning, I had my basic needs covered. I had my drugs, which was the most important thing for me, because I had to make sure I had enough drugs to get me through every day or evening, while making sure that I didn't overdose. Just keeping pace with cocaine would cost me R4000 a day. If I was taking cocaine, I wouldn't drink much alcohol, but drugs were key to my work: the more drugs, the better and more professional the strip show performance, plus the lap dance, plus the 'illegal' sex.

Competition between the girls over clients sometimes led to violent bashing of each other, and that was quite entertaining. I enjoyed watching the break-up fights with the girls in the dressing room.

And I also took part in these fights sometimes. I knew I was popular with the guys. I had regular clients, but I was sometimes also booked for a lap dance by other girls' clients after my shows. To get back at me, sometimes a girl would lie to a regular client of mine, saying I wasn't available so that he could book her. Their jealousy made me feel more desirable. Ayanda and I drifted apart though. Drugs do that to you – you become very close to people when you're high.

Did I feel good about myself?

I felt sexy, crazy, happy, high, the best stripper in the whole country. I felt that I could get anything I wanted.

This Eastgate mall club became very popular and opened branches in other towns where I also sometimes worked. I stayed with stripping for a couple of years, despite facing the occasional abuses by clients.

The original club was eventually closed down because it was raided by police, who arrested undocumented foreign girls from Japan and China, and South Africans who were stashing drugs.

But I stayed on in and around Johannesburg, and continued to strip in small clubs. After the club closed down, I spent some time working at clubs in smaller cities and towns in the strip club's network.

Getting hired in a 'white' strip club around that time was a long process. The club would thoroughly examine you to make sure your health was good, that you don't look like a druggie. Club owners always asked about my health, about what alcohol and drugs I took, what sex techniques I knew and so on.

Often, when I went for a new job, I'd get checked out by a doctor, and the girls had to go every three months for tests. A blood test would be taken, but I never got my results. After stripping, plus private lap dancing, plus sex, how would I know my infection status? The answer is that I never knew if I had an infection. I just knew that if the club owner came back to me, I was fine. If the owner didn't contact me, it may mean there was something wrong. They never said if we were sick or had HIV.

We never bothered to know more because we thought the greater danger was a drug overdose. We didn't know anything about ethics and responsibility. We didn't want to know our HIV status; we weren't told, and we didn't ask.

It would be club management who decided what work I

would do each night; I didn't get to choose. To impress the management, my skin needed to be baby-soft and smell nice, and so I always spent money on baby oil. The boss would check my flexibility, which was important for stripping on the pole. In this business, you get clients if your body looks good, not if you have a nice personality.

The condition of my body dictated whether I would be a stripper, a lap dancer, a nude waitress, and so on. These days it's different – workers have become more independent now in what they want to do at clubs. But I knew back then that these decisions were not up to me.

What we had learnt as black escort girls in the late 1990s, was that we had to be very careful and survive, because it was hard to find clubs that wanted us back then. And we needed the security of the clubs because those girls who were working for the pimps on the streets were often left desperate.

After a while working the clubs I decided that I needed to look for something more permanent.

Lisa was an agent for girls like us. She was a mature lady; her face was wrinkled, and she had blonde hair and green eyes. She was introduced to me as someone who could help me find new work. Lisa was obviously strong in the sex work networks operating at that time, recruiting girls like me – I knew that if I arrived somewhere new, I could use her name to get me through the door. It was like a recommendation.

I was twenty-two when I first moved from Joburg to Port Elizabeth, before my route took me back to Joburg, then on to Pietermaritzburg, then Durban and other small towns in KwaZulu-Natal, back to Joburg, and then to my final club in Port Elizabeth until I was twenty-six. Those were years lost in a haze of drugs and emotional dislocation.

Back then stripping was the only life I knew. Drugs were really all that mattered to me. Lisa said I should try a small club in Port Elizabeth where she had once worked.

I hitchhiked to Port Elizabeth using this method: I found a willing truck driver at a truck stop, gave him favours for the 'free' ride, arrived at the next truck stop, got cleaned up, got my drugs, found another trucker, gave him favours, and on it went. After I arrived in Port Elizabeth, I freshened up at the last garage, and then proceeded to the club Lisa had recommended.

This club was just stripping and lap dances. Regular guys could come and pay at reception to watch a show and go for a lap dance. I started working there as a stripper.

As I soon discovered, the other girls at this club were really young – some as young as sixteen. The youngest girls didn't do lap dancing, but only strip shows and pole dancing. For these girls, stripping was just an extra job, something fun they did in front of their boyfriends for drugs and smokes. They danced as if they were doing school gymnastics!

There were games in this club, and it was the pole dancers who competed for the most clients. Six girls would each dance on a table with a pole, performing her best moves. The guys would watch and cheer, moving around until they'd found who they thought was the best pole dancer. Then they'd shove cash into her panties. So one of the six girls would receive the most money, and then another six girls would start a new dance competition.

Then there were other girls, the older ones, walking around the floor, checking out which guys wanted a lap dance. Unnecessarily, in this club the girls would go nude in front of the clients.

I really didn't like this place because the client base was generally made up of white Afrikaans men, who were quite racist. I had to learn how to deal with their attitudes, and not act hostile or angry towards them, even though I hated the way they treated me. There were also always these crazy raids, with the cops coming into the club. Then everything would stop. Two hours later, everything would be back to normal again.

I soon knew that this club, with these young, inexperienced girls, just wasn't my scene. When a client told me I was too mature for the place, I returned to Johannesburg the same way I had come: via truckers on the prostitution route.

When I was back in Joburg, Lisa suggested I join a popular escort club in Pietermaritzburg. Getting there meant using the same trucking-prostitution strategy.

I eventually arrived at this club, where about eight of us girls had our own rooms in a quiet private house. The girls were all white, mostly from other countries, but they were friendly, and we all shared our drugs.

But this was another place whose crowds of white male clients didn't like black girls. In Joburg I had learnt to dance, to writhe on the floor and do various suggestive moves around a pole. But the clients here preferred the white chicks, apparently. I wondered why they had invited a black girl to perform there, when clearly the place was very white. The club and clients didn't like my style. It was also not very busy and I wasn't getting much money. I became a bit bored, so I decided to leave.

I spent the next few months travelling from one small KwaZulu-Natal town to another, finding clients, hustling rides with truck drivers, and keeping my drug habit going. I was gaining more experience as a hustler and a prostitute on the street again, a stripper in clubs and escort agencies when I could get that work, and a survivor on drugs.

If I needed more clients, I would ask a client in one club to refer me to other clubs. If I ended up getting a job at the new club, I would have to give the original client a service free of charge.

Trusting my client could also be risky though, and I could end up in the wrong hands. The client could take me to their own drug pimp, who would then make 'a deal' to use me: the pimp could claim that the client had brought me because he owed the pimp money. Then I was essentially 'bought', and I wouldn't receive any money for services I rendered while working for that pimp.

Escaping from a club I was not comfortable with sometimes meant moving to other towns and cities, and travelling was always risky. I always got into trouble going to unknown places. If I had a client, I could ask to be dropped at a club in Durban, but if I didn't know anyone there, I'd end up on the street. Or I might be dumped, and have to find my own way around in the middle of the night.

If I didn't have a client and was on the street late at night, a man could approach me and ask, 'Who's pimping you?' That's how you get into the wrong hands. There are pimps looking for girls like me on the streets, and I wanted to avoid them.

So I learnt to prostitute myself for transport with the truckers. After I had left a club, I'd walk the highways, hoping to get a ride to the nearest garage. There, I'd find another lift to the next garage, until I found a trucker who could take me further, sometimes all the way back to Joburg, in exchange for favours.

At the garages, I would change into my normal jeans and clothes. I would buy a gram of coke, some ecstasy and weed – enough to last me for a couple of hours on the highway. If I was going to get high, I had to be inside the truck, because being on the road was too dangerous.

Communication with the truckers was very easy: they knew what I needed, and vice versa.

'Where can I drop you?' a trucker would say, and we both knew that meant sex.

Sometimes it meant physical abuse as well.

It was a risk I took over and over again.

And I was feeling quite lonely and lost. I never had time to make friends in these places I was in. I was never anywhere for very long. I decided to return to Johannesburg to find work there. I would be less lonely there.

It was now 2003.

During this year on the streets and in the clubs of Joburg, I struggled on, feeding my drug habit. In the classier strip clubs I learnt how to dress nicely, knowing that I should not wear short skirts as this was the dress of the street girls.

At night I still preferred the safety net of the clubs, but in broad daylight I would hang around in malls, bars and restaurants, looking for clients. If you look like a prostitute during the day, in Midrand or Kempton Park, even your fellow prostitutes don't care that you are there. Instead of being in competition, the girls would challenge each other, because it was only the blow-job guys who wanted us during the day. It was money we earned to pay for our smokes.

But even so, it wasn't safe being a prostitute on the streets during the day. It was better, and safer, at night, when everyone was working: cops were out, pimps were out, girls were walking the streets, and ambulances were roving.

It could be dangerous during the day, when no one from our world was around. A guy could drive me far out of town, beat me up, then violently do his thing with me. I kept as safe as I could during the day by not dressing up too much, or exposing myself too obviously.

I just never understood how people could be so brutal.

Fifteen

AFTER I'D BEEN BACK IN Joburg a while, I met a guy who referred me to a nice club in Randburg.

It was early January in Joburg, summer-holiday time, and no one was around. Business had been very quiet, with just a few foreign tourists. This guy took me to the club, which was in an estate. It looked like a sports club, with a hotel for sports people who were visiting in town.

We entered the compound through high gates with security guards. On the fields nearby, men were playing sports. The cream walls of the large hotel building impressed me – it looked like a posh place with big, comfortable rooms.

Once we were in, I noticed that there were lots of German girls with long blonde hair living there. The guy explained that the men who were staying there were are on business, and that the girls gave massages.

It looked clean. It looked safe.

'So why are you bringing me here?' I asked.

'You can stay here for a while and work,' he replied.

I asked him, 'But what's in it for you, leaving me here?'

'Just say you're a chick from KZN and that you're not a working girl. I brought you here for an opportunity. You will get paid for it.'

I didn't get paid, and I spent three weeks inside this estate. I was given my own room, and I could find my own clients.

But I was not allowed to leave.

Because of the security, we couldn't even try to walk through the gates.

I discovered that the German girls were there because they were being 'taught' how to 'speak English'. That was the line, anyway. There were also some local Afrikaans- and English-speaking girls who were qualified strip workers. They hid themselves somewhere in the estate during the day.

At night, it was another ballgame.

The conference room of the estate turned into a swinging club, and all-night parties took place inside private rooms. The male clients had sex with each other as well. Drugs were everywhere. You could smoke anything you wanted – it was all there.

Where was I in all of this?

I was high on drugs, but this is the only time I can remember when only my boobs worked, not my cookie. The men liked massaging themselves between my large boobs, coming that way rather than through intercourse.

Trapped inside the estate, with nowhere to go, I became disgusted by the semen: it was all over my face and body. During my sex work, a guy would just grab my hair, and shove his thing into my mouth, then spill his semen all over my face.

So how did I get out of this big hotel estate finally? I had been there for three weeks. Then, one day, the hustler guy who initially brought me there arrived with a friend, another businessman, a black African from Ghana.

I had often felt sad about these African businessmen coming to South Africa. Local businessmen would approach me with money, and my job would be to entice their African business partners to sign a contract. This meant, for instance, that I had to get the African man so drunk that he would finally sign. It bothered me that I was part of the exploitation of others, when I had also been exploited.

This time, my original trafficker didn't recognise me as by now I had a changed my hair into a big Afro.

My plan for getting out of the estate was to seduce the Ghanaian guy and then get him to take me out. The problem was that when I asked him for a drink, he treated me as though I was a waitress, and said 'No, thank you.'

I tried to hint that I wasn't a bar lady trying to serve *him* a drink, that I was there for the same reason as all the other girls – the white girls.

It took a while to get through to him.

The image many men have of sex workers was portrayed by the German ladies with their long blonde hair and shiny white skin. Not by a voluptuous black woman with high, high heels and a contoured corporate dress that made her look like a sexy business woman. Mr Businessman was surprised by me.

I started to chat to him. He didn't know my background, so I told him a sob story about being dumped by my boyfriend, and that I could give him what he wanted far better than those white girls could. I tried to convince him to take me out with him, and I told him to tell his businessman friend, because I didn't want the whole thing to backfire.

My Ghanaian client eventually did what I asked. I don't know who he paid off, but he came to get me later, and took me out of the estate to his hotel. He was sweet with me, too. I felt like he took care of me, almost like a daughter.

It was done.

But I was left shocked after this experience of being a sex slave. So it was back to Joburg's streets, earning my own money for sex and thereby feeling that I was controlling my own drug habit.

When I was not working at an agency, I had my own South African clients and pimps. And again I had to try not to be controlled by the pimps. It's dangerous to try to get out of the pimp's hold on you, but it can be done with a willing client. He's also the guy I might ask to drive me out of town so I can avoid a pimp. It was often these clients who took me to the smaller clubs outside of the cities.

That's how many of my journeys began.

They would take me from Joburg to these clubs that played rock 'n' roll and old love songs. These places were too cozy for me, with mainly white Afrikaans guys who all knew each other. The women there worked as prostitutes and also handled the bar – usually, they basically ran these places. They were older women, too.

I would sometimes stay at a small-town club for a few days, but it never really lasted. As a black woman, I usually felt out of place at these clubs. I was just glad I had had the Port Elizabeth experience so I understood Afrikaners. For me back then, although it was unpleasant, I didn't take their words or actions as racist – I just understood them to be the influence of alcohol or drugs.

It was good that I could speak their language, although for many of those Afrikaners, it didn't matter – it was the colour of the skin that was important.

I would stay in these small towns for a few nights with different clients. Sometimes a client would get me a taxi in the morning to go wherever I had to go. I'd lie: 'My boyfriend dumped me, and I need money to get back home.' Then I would go to the town's nearest mall and hang out until the evening for more work. When I had enough money, I'd return to Joburg.

But truck transport often landed me in the wrong place. I'd try hitching a ride back to Joburg, and the driver would say he wasn't going there but could drop me at another club on his route.

Then I'd land at yet another boer club.

I remember walking into this small-town club once. I was all dusty, with old make-up on, and I walked up to the bar. The bar lady just looked at me and didn't say a word.

So I battered her with fluent Afrikaans. I knew she hadn't expected me to speak Afrikaans.

I had big, thick blonde braids at the time. She told me I was just a black whore, but probably a good one. She still had an attitude after that, but she became nicer. So I ordered a double brandy and Coke, an 'Afrikaner' drink, to show I knew I was on her 'turf'.

The place was dead. You could smell the dust. I heard a comment in Afrikaans from somewhere, 'O, *dit gaan baie donker wees in hierdie klub vanaand*' (Oh, it's going to be dark in this club tonight).

She asked me, 'Are you passing by?' and I started telling her about my issues. We chatted about that. As soon as she was comfortable with me, the guys took note, and the drinks started coming. My social light was on.

One man overheard us, immediately booked me and bought me drinks, which kept coming. When he left, I followed him to his car. He took me to his guest house, we had sex, and then we slept. I earned R300, I got an overnight stay, had a hot shower, was able to freshen up, and then had breakfast the next morning. I didn't think that was too bad.

That was the importance of making a good impression with the bar ladies.

But Johannesburg was becoming less kind to me – there was too much moving around, and every day was a battle, with new places and people, which meant I always had to be alert. I needed to settle with a club for a while where money was good. I was getting more professional, and I still needed to feed my drug habit.

What else was there for me?

I went to visit Lisa, who persuaded me to go back to Port Elizabeth to a more exclusive escort agency owned by Sunette. I had met Sunette in Port Elizabeth the first time I was there, and had heard about her posh escort strip club. Lisa suggested that

I had a good chance of working there now.

Outside Johannesburg I walked on the highways and then hitchhiked with several lorry drivers to Port Elizabeth. In return for the rides, the drivers received my services, but some of them abused me. They had a bad tendency of spitting on me, and they often told me they thought that what I was doing was disgusting.

After having sex, one trucker spat on me, saying I was a useless woman. I still remember his saliva on my face – another blow to my fragile self-esteem.

When I arrived at Sunette's escort agency in central Port Elizabeth, I found a dreary building squashed between two double-storey houses on a small street. It was painted blue on the outside and had a black roof. A sign outside read 'Lounge Bar'. It wasn't very inviting, not what I had expected from this upmarket club. The windows were painted black.

Inside was a downstairs bar/lounge, and tables with poles. Upstairs, clients could use the themed rooms for their entertainment – there were Indian- or Asian-themed rooms, and rooms with different colour schemes.

I found out later that most of the clients were Afrikaners engaged in the trading of perlemeon, so money was always forthcoming.

I had never stayed for very long in any other place, but I ended up being employed by this escort agency for three years, until I was twenty-six.

The club was quiet and had more mature ladies. While I was there, I managed to have my own place to stay, although I was not permitted to have clients at my place, and I had some freedom and some protection. All of us girls who worked there had our own advertising in newspapers and on websites, and when we weren't working we were mostly inside the escort agency waiting to be picked up. I could also be contacted on my cellphone by clients who had read my adverts.

Sunette's club gave me the personal security I had been craving – I felt safe. But my income wasn't that stable as it depended on how many clients I had. I never knew how much money I would get, so I had to go easy with my drugs. It was easy enough to get them, though – nearby, I could buy coke, weed, anything.

Apart from condoms, I never used protection against pregnancy. Some clients would give more money if they didn't use a condom. But now that I was there, I wasn't concerned about anything other than getting high.

When I arrived at the escort agency every evening, I would already be high on coke. Then I would take a blue ecstasy tablet. Ecstasy lasts a long time in the system and, along with my drinks, would hold me over from 7pm to midnight. There are different strengths of the drug: green, blue and white, with green the strongest and white the weakest.

During the early-evening hours, my mind would be reeling, trying to prepare for the night's clients. But the escort agency would be quiet, and that's when I would play on the poles with my songs, working on new moves, just enjoying it.

I had always loved stripping. I was on the pole every minute I could be. This kept my body very firm, and made me feel sexy. I'd entertain myself by grabbing a pole and wrapping my body around it, dancing to the music.

That's why I enjoyed stripping: it took my mind out of the escort agency.

Sunette was an Afrikaans lady in her late thirties. She

was chubby, with dark hair, and was very confident. She was protective about our safety because she knew she needed us for business. She was also an aggressive negotiator, both with the girls and with clients. Nobody messed with Sunette! Sometimes, regular clients would chat with Sunette at the bar for a while, maybe to make friends – but a new client didn't get to have social chats with the boss.

She didn't negotiate with clients on price. If the client didn't want to pay for a full hour, then she would tell them to go away. If they then said they only wanted half an hour, she wouldn't agree either, because she knew that the Viagra would last an hour anyway. Some guys thought they could negotiate pricing this way, but Sunette didn't play around: she'd state up front what had to be paid, no cutting corners.

When they were talking about me, I once overheard a footballer say, 'But she's a black chick,' as though I was worth less money than the white girls. I told Sunette that I won't go with this client if I was going to be insulted like that. She was mostly interested in the cash, though: she told me not to worry as the guy would have to pay up front.

Sunette was clever. I might complain about having to go out to do a strip show when I'd rather go on a booking with a client, because travelling to an outside strip show was not paid time – I could earn more money having lots of clients than I could doing one strip show outside the escort agency. When we complained, she shut us up by giving us drugs. The drugs worked and we'd end up doing what she wanted anyway. When she liked our work, she'd give us a bottle of alcohol as a reward.

The bookings went like this:

Sex meant intercourse or penetration. A blow job was a

different fee. Lap dance was touch-and-feel while dancing naked, but no sex. If the client wanted to climax, he had to pay me extra, right there and then, and that became my money. The anal fee was higher, and involved penetration – I never did that one. It was left to the girls who couldn't get other clients. If a client paid R600 for a short session, I needed to be prepared to give him the works, and he would decide along the way. A threesome was two girls and one guy; it brought in R700 an hour, which we girls split.

There was a girl at the agency, Tammy, who started to perform threesomes with me. Sometimes a client wanted a white and a black girl to satisfy a fantasy. Or Tammy and I would play, offering the client the impression of being innocent and young. Tammy had long black hair but a boyish body – she looked like a rock star. I would rub my skin with oil mixed with black hair spray so it was a shiny pitch-black, and my hair would be pulled back flat as if it was shaved. We'd 'play' like this, with the lights dimmed.

A fantasy booking meant playing a character; it cost more since clothes and room decoration was involved. Some of the fantasies I had to play were being a young girl, an innocent young Afrikaans girl on a farm, or being raped by an uncle. I felt I had enough experience to make this look realistic, and I relied on my drugs to stop my emotions from overwhelming me.

It's a competitive business, so I had to learn how to keep my clients happy, how to satisfy them, so they would keep coming back to me. I could give a massage as an 'extra', and there were also clients who wanted you to swallow when they ejaculated – that needed an extra payment as well. We weren't supposed to do this, because all money was supposed to go through the escort agency. Some regular clients were on credit, so Sunette would lose money if they didn't pay her directly for a booking.

If a regular client wanted to negotiate price with me once we were alone in the room, and didn't pull out his money, I would say no. If he asked for extra first without showing he intended to pay, I wouldn't even bother – I took it as an indication that he might tell our secrets to the boss.

But if a regular or a new client put out the cash so I can see it, then I would go ahead and give him extra service anyway. No words said. I could get into trouble with the agency management if I encouraged such clients, but my excuse was that I didn't know if a client had already paid for the booking or not.

For new clients, we girls would see if he had money to spend by giving more than what he had booked for. After fifty minutes, the boss would knock on the door to indicate that time was nearly up. It was then, in the last five or so minutes of the hour-long session, when the client was about to get dressed and while his trousers were still open, that the extra service was given. She'd then get the extra cash directly from him. But with regular clients, we would do what they had booked for, unless they first showed their cash up front. And we never talked about it.

You can also get clients who wanted to get their service in private areas, or in cars, or with violence. I never used to fight them back, because by then I expected it. I lived each day for the drugs alone – violence was the price I felt I had to pay to feed my habit.

We girls spent a lot of time naked, both at the agency and when we were at home resting. On Sundays especially, we girls were always nude, pampering our bodies to make them clean and soft.

Stripping at the club required a lot of energy drinks because we didn't eat much while we were working. Because of that and the drugs, we developed pimples. So Sundays were our days to put lemon juice on our pimples so that they healed, and we'd drink lots of water to cleanse ourselves.

Sundays were also Windhoek beer days. We would have 24s of Windhoek beer, which we'd then pour into a bath. Flipping through beauty magazines we'd collected or stolen from doctors' rooms, we'd bath ourselves in this Windhoek magic, sometimes sharing two or three girls to the bath, soaking ourselves until our skin was baby soft.

This Port Elizabeth escort agency had various ways of creating hype and making extra money, and one of these was holding competitions.

The owner came up with a few sex games to turn on the clients. Sometimes a client would have come into the club and seen the strip show by 1am. To get the most cash out of the clients, the club owner designed these games for the later hours, 3 or 4am, when everyone was high, so that clients would get interested all over again, and make a new booking.

One game involved holding a burning cigarette in your cookie while holding your legs up and open. We'd be on our bums with our hands on the floor, legs wide open in the air holding the cigarette without it falling. Sometimes the cigarette would go out, so someone would come and light it again. And some of the girls were too drunk to keep holding the cigarette. This game turned on some clients big time. They would catcall and root for you to keep going. It made the guys so horny and they loved it!

We'd get burnt a lot, but as a result of this game, the muscles in my vagina became very strong, which worked for me.

Another way of making more money was for the clients to buy body shots. I would lie naked on the bar and the clients' drinks were put on my body, on my nipples and cookie. I had to be sure my body was well covered with baby oil. As they took the shots from my body, they would buy more drinks and get drunk faster. If a client booked me, I'd get off the bar top and go off with him.

These games were always done at the end of the month, when money flowed.

Sunette's agency was unusually good for gaining stripping experience because part of the business was to advertise for shows at outside venues.

Most of the time, outside bookings were for strip shows, mainly at bachelor parties. End-of-year parties kept us very busy as many guys got married then. We girls made a lot of money from strip shows then, but I would never know where I was going.

In November 2005 a football team from West Africa was in town to play in the Nelson Mandela Challenge, and one night half of them arrived at our escort agency. That night, I shook my body at them as I swung round the pole. When they saw me, the only black chick in the club, they immediately booked me for two days at their hotel. I was happy that these African men wanted a black girl, and I felt honoured by the colour of my skin. I was glad they were tired of watching the white women.

They paid up front, and the next night the bouncer and driver took me to their hotel. I was worried, though, because my drug supply was low.

The whole team was there, and my jaw was very active that

night – they all wanted blow jobs.

And then my jaw became locked while I was doing a blow job. When I cried out in pain, the guy just went ahead with his mission, and spilled sperm all over my face. What a freak! Thankfully, he was the second last guy to have me.

Our bar lady from the agency, Tracy, was called to come help. She walked in the room and punched me hard on both of my cheeks to release my jaw. Then we put a lot of ice on my face and down my throat.

When I told them I was done for the night, the oldest guy in the team said he wanted to book me out again.

It was different for officials, community leaders, public figures, fat cats and politicians. They never came to the escort agency themselves, but they'd send an official. You're booked and you go, never knowing where to.

When I got to a VIP's house, we'd negotiate whether he wanted an hour over and above the booking. If so, and before I undressed, he would pay me directly. I would call the agency to report that he had booked for an extra hour, and then I'd give the money to the bouncer, who'd deliver it to the agency later. This kept me safe and secured me more money. And I'd know the bouncer and driver would be outside. The MPs or official who booked me would also often give me extra cash after it all was finished.

Someone at the University of Port Elizabeth once booked me for a strip show that was for young male graduates and some teachers. I had to perform in the middle of a very big hall, and I had taken the blue ecstasy tablet to help me, because I knew there would be lots of people.

There was only a little light in the room, and I used candle wax, with another girl pouring it on me. During a strip show, I would always observe the faces in the crowd in case they wanted to find me and book me later. But these guys just gasped and went 'Yoh, yoh!' in utter surprise! They didn't seem to know anything about stripping or that black strippers even existed.

These guys weren't turned on and they weren't even horny – just totally shocked! To think I had taken a blue tablet just to shock them!

Sixteen

PART OF THE RISKINESS OF prostitution – even when it's organised with an escort club – was allowing a paying client to beat me up, hurting my body. I let the abuse happen. This is why it was better to be high when I let a client have his way with me – it's part of the reason why drugs were so important to me. I couldn't have done my job otherwise.

The escort agency had rules, though. One of them was that we were not supposed to smoke the client's coke with the client: you did so at your own risk. I had my own stash of drugs, but when I was in a private club room, it was a risk I took. I was not going to sit at the bar without a client. So if a client wanted to abuse me, I'd let it happen as long as he provided the drugs.

It was all kept quiet, because we were both breaking the rules. But if I didn't let him do what he wanted with me and that made him unhappy with me, he could tell the boss that we were coking in the room. Then, I'd be in trouble.

That's the power of money and drugs.

Another reason why the club needed rules was that a client could actually be a cop trying to catch out the club for having drugs. That's why I would ask a new client to take off all his clothes and have sex first, before I took any drugs with him. Then he wouldn't be able to lock me up because he'd already had sex with me – I could have said that he had raped me. My logic was that he could not pay at the club reception for a sexual service, and then lock me up for drugs.

We assessed new clients by figuring out whether any of the girls already knew him, and using our own intuition about whether he was 'real' or an undercover cop. If a client was someone we didn't know, someone who'd just dropped into the club for the first time, then we wouldn't mess with him or his drug stash.

I once had a client who was a cop, and when I went to untie his trousers, he immediately showed resistance. I then felt his badge and pistol. I stopped what I had been doing.

'If you're not going to have sex, then you can get a refund,' I said. I left the private room 'to get a cigarette' and gave a sign to the club management that I was with a cop.

At other times, someone would tip off the cops that there were drugs at the club, and then the cops would raid. And so we girls were arrested a lot. We'd laugh about having 'a rest', which meant going to a jail cell to get some sleep.

We were usually dressed in our bikinis when we were picked up, and only sometimes did we manage to grab a jacket as we were herded by the police out of the club.

With our hands handcuffed behind our backs, we would plead with the cop: 'Please, wrap the jacket around my shoulders, please, please, please ...!' It was so cold outside in our little bikinis!

The owners of the club would bring out their lawyers. We girls in the jail would tell the lawyers that if they didn't bail us out, we would talk: we'd disclose that the club did have drugs. In the end, the owners would use money we had earned to bail us out – so we lost that income. It was cruel that they did that; it felt like punishment. When we were let out of the cells the next day, the club owners would just give us a packet of cigarettes, R100 and one gram of coke. But the money for our labour was gone. Of course the owners themselves were never caught. I don't know why.

We were once taken to court for having drugs, but there was no trial because the cops couldn't find the actual drugs at the bar. Most of the time, we girls wouldn't bring our own coke to the clubs – instead, we would just pop ecstasy tablets.

It was only Tracy, our bar lady, who would hide coke behind the bar. It was brought to the club by these tall Afrikaner guys who carried out illegal abalone harvesting. They would always arrive high, with their hair still wet from their dives in the ocean, and they would stay the whole night. The cops were always looking for these guys.

Seventeen

WHILE I WAS AT SUNETTE'S agency, I had one cool guy, a regular client and a rich one, who had started to book me at his house. He had another girl at the club, Tammy, who did threesomes with me. Until he met me he'd never known there was a black girl at the agency.

Among the girls, we had this thing that we never spoke about our clients if we thought we were falling in love with them. We had to stay neutral. But Tammy would talk about this guy all the time, and how good he was towards her. She kept bragging about him, how he was so nice, taking her for dinner and talking to her for hours.

This irritated me, so I told Tammy that he was also very good in bed! She was shocked – she'd thought she was his only girl. So I carried on. I bragged about him and his sexual antics. When Tammy learnt that he seemed to prefer me, she got jealous, but I competed with her and won his preferences: he kept booking me and not her for three weeks.

This is the kind of thing that would make the girls betray each other. The club didn't have a policy about the girls harassing each other. So, in this kind of situation, the other girl would try to destroy anything of mine, like my lingerie and even my reputation.

It worked like that. Even the client enjoyed the drama.

By my second year at the club, I was used to many different types of clients, but some are more memorable than others.

A black priest and his wife once booked me in the 'Queen' room, which had a rich gold-and-brown colour scheme. I guess the priest wanted royal sex. He even arrived wearing his white collar!

He was very upset with his wife because she had told him that she didn't want sex. She had two reasons: firstly because she felt pious about their sexual relationship, and secondly because she thought he had been cheating on her. I wondered why they had chosen to deal with these issues at the escort agency. I was already high on drugs when I met them, and they were very sober.

'What will make my wife want to have sex with me?' the priest pleaded.

So I tried to make them horny, and started dancing, slowly. He reacted by taking off his collar. I stopped and told them to get comfortable because they would enjoy what was coming. I could see the wife was angry and uncomfortable – she was very stiff. I took her hand and moved it towards her husband, helping her touch him, and she slowly became interested. Soon they started caressing each other and I left them alone to enjoy themselves.

'Another successful day at the office,' I said to myself, relieved that there'd been no sex for me.

Those were the kinds of moments when I enjoyed my job.

And then there was 'Greek', a very depressed, weird guy.

He'd book me for two hours, and he would bring the coke. We might cuddle a bit, or I'd massage him. And then he would start talking about his wife, how she didn't do the things he asked, or he'd wonder aloud what she would like, whether or not she would want someone else in the room during sex. Stuff like that. I never understood why he would want us to get high, and then just sit and smoke in the room, talking and talking.

I found that Greek had lots of emotional issues, and he used me as a sounding board. It was good money, but I wasn't his counsellor and our sessions put me on edge.

I had to take his coke, because if I didn't, it would look as though I was going to cheat or rob him. And I knew I always had to be sensitive to his needs, otherwise he would complain to the club, and the boss might slap me to get into line. But Greek was so boring. And because I was bored, I would have to add more ecstasy or smoke more weed, just to keep my energy levels up for the night's next client.

Sometimes he could not have an erection when I massaged him, and this worried me because this is what I did professionally! My job was to satisfy my client. I tried some stunts, like asking him if he'd like to be tied up, or if we could bring in another girl for a threesome.

Anything to be more active, because unless I was physically active, doing my thing with the client, my drugs would cause me great discomfort. I was used to getting high before I met a client – that's the only way I could pull off a 'good heist'. So by the time I had taken coke with Greek, I would be sweating – the coke in my head would make me horny and I'd have to find ways of calming down my body.

With Greek, I would sometimes have to take two cold showers during our talking sessions – just to cool down. I would have to tell Greek that I was using the bathroom.

Although we mostly talked, sometimes Greek would come to the club already high. Then he'd be rough with me, slapping me and throwing me against the wall. He'd shout at me, making me act as though I was his wife.

'Why don't you want to go on vacation with me? You said you wanted a break!' he would shout, then slap me.

'No! No!' I would fake cry.

That's how he acted out his anger.

Did I like prostituting myself?

When I was high on drugs, I felt horny myself. By this time I was not only addicted to drugs, but to sex itself. I had become a sex addict. And I wanted to do a good job – I felt satisfied when a client climaxed.

'I'm not here to drink tea with you,' I would say.

The lifestyle could be fun, sometimes. I liked it when the agency would send us out to buy new lingerie for a particular strip show. I liked when I was walking through a shopping mall and someone recognised me as a stripper. Sure, I liked this lifestyle.

But there are emotions that come out when you're in your

own space. That's when the memories come back. When I was alone in my room, and not high, these memories would haunt me. I would fight myself back and forth:

'I shouldn't be doing this ... but I know why I'm doing it.'

'I'm not normal. I cannot go out there and be normal.'

'I can't go home to my mom.'

'Ntombi would say I knew what I was getting into ...'

Lousy memories.

Eighteen

KERRI WAS ONE OF THE girls who worked in the club, and I struck up a friendship with her. She was a tall white girl with freckles on her face, and she had long, silky brown hair. Her feet and legs were nice and smooth, like a football player's. We performed a threesome for a client, and I enjoyed having sex with Kerri. I actually became fond and protective of her, even though I didn't know her very well, and that was a first for me.

People in the club disliked that Kerri and I were getting close and hanging out together. Friendships like that weren't really encouraged.

I remember saying I would visit her at her house, not knowing she lived right across from our boss, Sunette. I was surprised to find that Kerri still lived with her parents, who charged her rent to stay there. Kerri couldn't understand why we couldn't hang out together – she was OK with me visiting.

Kerri accidentally fell pregnant. Sunette said that she should have the baby and Sunette would provide the childcare. I had heard that Sunette could not have children of her own. I just had a strange feeling about this. I didn't trust the situation.

Kerri worked as a stripper up to her ninth month of pregnancy. I became the protective, emotional girlfriend. We hung out on Saturday afternoons when we weren't working, and we had a baby shower, which was nice.

She gave birth to a baby boy.

Then Kerri's heart turned around. When the baby was nine months old, she gave the baby to Sunette to care for. Sunette would bring the baby to the club and brag about him to everyone.

And this upset Kerri. She changed her mind again, and asked Sunette to give the baby back. I don't know what happened, but Sunette was very upset. Kerri left the club with her baby.

I never heard Sunette speak about the baby again, but I was heartbroken to lose such a special friend.

Then came Elton, a handsome, classy coloured man who enjoyed cricket. We started seeing each other outside of the club, although I knew he had a wife and daughter, and another girlfriend. I knew that I was not allowed to have a client as a boyfriend, but I felt very comfortable with Elton because he was so kind to me.

He would come to the club and pay R350 for an hour just

so that I could rest. We would kiss and fondle sometimes, but mostly he let me sleep. I got to the point where I really thought I was in love with this guy.

He knew Sundays were my off days, and so he would pick me up from my place in his black Jetta, in which he always played his favourite Toni Braxton songs. We would go out for breakfast, followed by walks on the beach. Elton would make Sundays a lot of fun.

Of course we had sex – I felt I owed him that since he paid for my rest time at the club – but not very often. He also didn't allow me to take drugs in front him, so I would always get high before we met up.

I didn't have a phone, so I never knew when he would come to fetch me. I just had to wait for him, and I'd get anxious when a week went by and I hadn't seen or heard from him. Then, he would suddenly arrive on a Friday night, and book me so I could sleep. We agreed that he shouldn't walk out after a session, but stay at the bar for a while so it looked legitimate.

As time went on and this became the norm, I started getting furious at him for leaving me for so long all week. To get back at him for being so silent during the week, I would try book another client before he booked me. This went on for months. When we were in the room together, we wouldn't have sex but would end up arguing.

'You didn't even come by to see me last Sunday,' I would tell him.

'Can I pick you up later tonight?' he would ask.

'What? Of course not!' I'd retort, angrily. 'Don't you know I'm a whore? I can't do that!'

Elton had a steady job working as the general manager at a

large food chain store. He also had a club in one of the local townships outside Port Elizabeth. Sometimes, after my work, he would pick me up and take me to his club. This was dangerous because club managers circulate around the clubs to see if their girls are picking up other clients. So I would wear a crazy hair weave so I wouldn't be spotted. Or I would hide under the DJ tables, where I could give him a blow job as he stood by.

Elton excited me and I fell for him.

He told me a lot about himself, but I never discussed myself.

In the escort agency, all of us girls discussed the fact that some clients really grew to like us. But also, I wondered, if a client really cared, then why didn't he make me his girlfriend and let me leave this business?

'Oh, here comes my boyfriend!' one girl would say.

'Oh, please. If he's your boyfriend, then why doesn't he rescue you from this hellhole?' another would reply. And it was true. We girls would talk about this among ourselves.

And there came a time when we all started getting fed up with the club. Girls were starting to leave. For me, working at the escort agency was getting boring. I was getting tired of it all, tired in all the busyness. Every week, the cops would raid the club, looking for people selling drugs. We'd get locked up half naked, and have to pay bail from our own funds.

Elton was the main reason I stayed in Port Elizabeth for so long. He was my last client before I discovered I was pregnant. I was twenty-six by then, and I discovered I was pregnant when I was about three of four months along. And I started to enjoy this life inside me.

That's when I started to thinking things could change. I felt like I could be a woman. I thought, wow, I still have time to do this mothering thing. I still have time to change.

I wanted to keep the baby and I started calling it Summer, but agency management said no – when I told Sunette I was pregnant, she told me coldly that the club could not continue to employ me unless I had an abortion.

Confused, I thought about how they had allowed Kerri to keep her baby and continue working, both during *and* after her pregnancy.

Sunette said she had a solution for me. Abortion. She didn't care about my opinion.

She had complete authority over my life. When someone in this business has that kind of authority, they are not thinking about your life. They are not thinking about your heart, about what is best for you. They are only thinking about your body, and they'll tell you straight out that you are not going to bring issues like this into their business.

So she told me that I had to abort the baby. And I thought to myself, look, you're obviously going to be killed here.

The abortion was done that same day, and it was done forcibly. I protested, so I was drugged.

That day, seeing Summer's tiny legs in the sink next to me made me feel like I was murdering someone. Afterwards I bled a lot and I was told to just put a sponge in my private parts to stop the bleeding. That same evening I was told to take a client.

While I was waiting, half naked in my lingerie at the bar, I saw this guy coming towards me. And something in my aching gut just said no.

I just couldn't do it. And that was the day I said, 'This is it.'

When you say no to a pimp, that's when you get killed. But I decided that day to say no to Sunette. When I said it out loud, the club bouncers beat me up so badly that I collapsed. They probably also gave me injections to put me out, because I remember nothing after that.

I don't even remember when they drove me from Port Elizabeth to Johannesburg and dumped me. I was found on Bree Street in Joburg and taken to the hospital. When I woke up several weeks later, both my body and my mind were damaged.

In the hospital, I was visited by a kind nun, who prayed for me while I was there, and then took me to a Catholic rehabilitation centre for drug addicts. I hardly knew this nun, and in my state I hardly ever spoke to her, but I think she saved my life.

At the drug rehab centre I got very sick on their detox programme – I had the shakes, emotional fits and a runny tummy. When I had the shivers, craving for a drug, my mind would think of devilish ways to get coke.

In those first three weeks of rehabilitation, not taking coke or any other drugs and not having sex was not too difficult for me because I had made up my mind to change. I still had my cigarettes and weed, and my heart was aching for change.

But mostly, for about five months after the forced abortion, I was out of it. I don't remember much except that I was in and out of hospital during this time, and had to take tablets to keep me calm. And I felt like I was in a mad house. I was not myself.

Did I contemplate suicide? Oh my goodness, yes!

I hadn't been suicidal after I gave birth to Z, and after I'd given him up for adoption. I had hurt very badly, but I was younger and I'd had my drugs afterwards to soothe me. But I was suicidal after I lost Summer. And I was not on drugs this time – this time, during my rehabilitation, the emotional pain was strong. There was nowhere I could hide from my pain; I had to face it.

Mostly, I just wanted to die.

There were times during my hospital stays that I took off the bed sheet and tied it around my neck. I would tie the other end to the bed, hoping to fall off during sleep and be choked. The dreams I had were all about falling into a dark hole. But I never fell off the bed.

And I kept coming back to the same thought: that this abortion had been forced upon me. I'd had no choice. That it was part of this trafficking story.

I had lost my Summer, another baby, to this lifestyle.

I told myself then that I didn't want to do clubbing and prostitution any more. After my drug rehab, the nun who had cared for me looked for a safe place for me to stay. She placed me in a shelter.

Margaret, the Zulu sister I knew from my first experiences on Hillbrow's streets eight years earlier, somehow heard my story and came to see me at that shelter. She was the first person from outside the rehab programme that I had seen since arriving back in Joburg. I was very quiet and not responsive – I just stared at her, wondering why she was visiting me. Mostly, at that time, I got irritated by people being in my space. I just wanted to be alone and quiet.

There were a few people in the shelter who slowly started to look familiar, but I didn't care. We had group sessions, but I wouldn't say anything, just listen to other people's stories. They were stories about drugs, not prostitution. But I guess those stories encouraged me to push forward at least, to keep breathing.

As I got stronger, I was taken for training in making things, and I was taken to other rehabilitation centres. But in all that time, I had nothing to say to anybody. I remained quiet, my mind switched off.

Isolated.

This went on for over a year.

After a while I felt the need to be on my own and I left the shelter. I took to the parks, sleeping out, looking for a place to live. I had been off drugs for about a year by now, and I had no money. I went to churches for food and ate it in the parks. Doing this I could, at least, get through the day. Sleeping in parks each night, I actually really didn't care what happened to me.

After living on the street, and wandering around for about a year, I found a new shelter which included a soup kitchen. The shelter was part of a church programme. That's how I met the Houghton Methodists.

I decided to go to the church, even though I found the people irritating. There was lots of jumping up and down, praying loudly and singing, and loud talking. There was very little peace and silence. At least the nuns were quiet and didn't say much to me – they seemed more spiritual.

In this new church, people welcomed me but I had always thought of myself as an independent person, a person who didn't need help or interference, so I found it very hard to make any friends. People picked up on my attitude, and tried to draw me out. But I wasn't ready to be approached or embraced in such a friendly manner. They thought I was being anti-social.

The ladies at the church irritated me, because I felt they used their 'charity' to control others. I got annoyed because even after all that had happened, I still had my pride. I felt they were condescending, with all their talking.

'I hope you don't smoke again.'

'Why aren't you wearing that nice dress we gave you?'

'How are you feeling now ...?'

Too many questions. And so my responses were cocky. I hadn't realised that getting a plate of food meant giving out details of my whole life.

I did sit down with a psychologist to tell my story, and I trusted her because she was a member of the church. But I felt no consolation in her attempts to move me forward – I continued to carry with me the trauma of my forced abortion. We only had two sessions. I don't know why. Perhaps I was not ready to confront my traumas and the stigma attached to me, a homeless and decrepit young woman grovelling around on the streets of Joburg.

The church had developed a form that stated where the people using the soup kitchen came from. The purpose was to collect money to send us home at Christmas. I didn't accept this gesture, because the problem was this: if they give you a ticket 'home', and you're indigent and family-less, where do you go when you get there?

The Methodists really tried to help, but nothing was working.

I had lost trust in people. Period. I couldn't do this friendly thing with them. All I wanted was to be left alone.

Eventually I was told by the shelter that I was strong now, and that perhaps I should leave and look for my own place.

Because she had visited me in hospital, and because she was the only friend I could think of, I decided to look for Margaret to see if I could stay with her for a few days. I found her place in Hillbrow, but she wasn't there. Her friend said I could stay for two nights. The place was so familiar, with the street life, the drugs, but I never did find Margaret.

I continued sometimes to look for my other old Joburg friends. At the end of every day's wandering I would go back to the Hillbrow girls to see how they were doing. Some of them had pimps, and wanted a 'trust-thing' with me. I hung around their flat, cleaning it for them, but I didn't want to go back to my old way of life, to their way of life.

And I couldn't stay long with them because they often brought clients home. They told me that if I wasn't doing the night work, it wouldn't look right for me to stay there. So it was always back to sleeping in parks.

Other than that, I didn't have much to distract me. My baby Z was more on my mind than ever before, even though I had never known him.

And at the back of my mind, I was thinking about how the Methodists might be able to provide an answer for my weary soul's searching for a better life. It just hadn't been the right time. I intended to return because, despite my issues, at the church I had felt for the first time that I had met my spiritual self.

Nineteen

My mother was also on my mind.

Slowly I had realised that I needed to get out of this situation I had found myself in, and stop blaming people for what had happened to me. The bruises from the beatings and waking up in the hospital, all the time wandering from one street or shelter to another, with no support – all these things made me want to change.

I decided to return to my mother in Cape Town, to see if I could make my way, to start some sort of 'new life' away from the immediate past. I was now nearly twenty-eight, and I hadn't been back to Cape Town since the age of eighteen; ten years before.

But to get to Cape Town, I needed money.

I started sliding back into my old habits. I knew outlets in central Johannesburg which pushed drugs around the country, so I took up one offer and flew to Cape Town for a drop.

There, I reunited with my mother. She was still in the same house in Khayelitsha, where she lived with my two half-brothers. Richard had died by then. But in that house it felt like I was nine years old again. From the very beginning, my mother and I fought a lot: it was the same scene over and over again. She was just interested in the money, and she encouraged me to go back to prostitution to make money to support us both.

My way was becoming unclear again – I became confused about my purpose and my spirit. I had been trying to ease my way back into a society I had never really been part of.

But with the pressure and the fighting and the pain and the fear, my drug habit raised its ugly head again.

Taking drugs means paying for drugs, and as soon as the drugs were in my system, I fell back on my profession of stripping and prostitution.

One night, while visiting the strip clubs in Cape Town, looking for clients, I was invited into a network run by a leading ANC politician, Mr M. He helped organise 'lounges' for VIPs in and out of Cape Town, with us girls carrying out strip shows and serving clients.

It was there that I met and befriended Lindiwe. A skinny, very proud Xhosa woman with short hair which she sometimes wore in a weave or braids, Lindiwe looked like a model. Her dangling earrings and fashionable African designer clothes highlighted her smooth brown skin. I was happy for her that she wanted to make it on TV. She was younger than I was, about twenty-one, and we plied around Cape Town's strip joints together.

Lindiwe had never visited Joburg and she had dreams of going there. She had heard about this Methodist church all the TV celebrities attended, and she wanted to go there. She didn't know that it was the same Methodist church that had helped rehabilitate me after the painful Port Elizabeth abortion, and that I intended to return to them.

So we both had spiritual goals. And while we were waiting to fulfil them, Lindiwe and I moved about Mr M's VIP lounges. Mr M particularly liked me and we spent one night in bed, but he was so drunk that we never had sex. When he woke up, he assumed we had, and remarked, 'Oh, you know what? I don't think we used a condom.' He gave me R500 and told me to buy a morning-after tablet. I was thinking all along how I needed the money for my mom, just to keep her quiet.

But I blackmailed Mr M for several months after that.

I convinced him I was pregnant with his child and wanted to keep the baby. In my whole life, I'd never had a bank account until I met him. But he felt sorry for me and paid me a monthly allowance directly into a bank account he set up for me.

He also tried to convince me to have an abortion, thinking his reputation would be at stake. When I refused, Mr M told me, 'Please, I need you to show me your pregnancy results every month.'

I found another pregnant woman friend, and told her: 'Take your urine to the lab and get a copy of the test. I'll pay you R100 a month.'

On the original urine test results each month, I Tipp-Exed out her name and stuck my own typed name onto it, then faxed the photocopy off to Mr M, who was based in Joburg.

Seven months into the fake pregnancy, I was still receiving funds from him, as he had promised.

'Now I need to buy baby clothes, shoes and bedding,' I explained to him.

And he sent me more money.

After the 'birth', Mr M asked to see photos of the baby.

'But I have twins!' I said, thinking that I could get double the money.

The problem arose when I couldn't find any mother with recent twins to photograph. Nor did my proxy pregnant friend have twins. He had been sending me about R1 800 a month, but I now asked for between R7 000 and R8 000 for baby clothes and my own care.

He kept asking to see the 'babies'. I started avoiding his calls and acting funny. I told him he must come to Cape Town to meet my mother, who demanded that he pay lobola for me.

That's when he went quiet. When he stopped his pursuit, I started calling him, even sending him threatening SMSes. He knew that if he didn't pay up, I could bring his case to the media, or to his family.

I received another allotment of money.

It was not the right thing to do, but his money helped me avoid more prostitution.

PART 3

Twenty

AFTER MY FAKE PREGNANCY, I had money and I decided to try to live clean again – I was still taking drugs, but I had no sex with anyone for about a year.

Instead, I worked as a waitress at Harry's Pancakes at the V&A Waterfront. My friend Lindiwe also found work there, and we did some stripping on and off, while working at Harry's Pancakes in the day. Eventually Lindiwe left for Joburg to follow her dreams.

After work, my fellow girl co-workers and I used to go out to town for some fun. I wasn't interested in picking up any guy or hustling because of my strict no-sex diet. But one evening, we girls decided to see what we could 'catch'. The clubs on Long Street did not have entrance fees, so you just went in, showed yourself and met whoever you met.

That's when I met Charles from DRC. This tall, handsome black guy with bright eyes, pronounced lips and broad shoulders seemed so different from other men I had known. He came over to me with his good English and started chatting, telling me he worked as a barman at another bar.

'I don't chat with guys unless they buy me a drink,' I told him, flippantly.

He left.

I sat at the bar and watched my friends dancing. About half an hour later, Charles reappeared with a drink in his hand.

We chatted. He kept buying drinks, but I didn't want to drink much since I was smoking weed. We ended up dancing and having a lot of fun. That night we went to his place in town, where he slept on a mattress on the floor.

I hadn't had sex for a whole year, but sex was fun with him. Charles could act manly and arrogant, but he was also sweet.

We saw more of each other.

Within three months, we had developed a liking for each other. I wasn't interested in a serious relationship, but it was nice having a boyfriend, like my friends did, and having sex for fun. We never discussed love or our feelings towards each other, even though I eventually left Khayelitsha and moved in with him at his place.

At first I was careful to always use a condom.

But gradually, we went off it.

Twenty-one

EVENTUALLY I FELL PREGNANT AND had to tell Charles, not just about the pregnancy but about my past; I told him everything. I told him that I'd already had two pregnancies. I also told him I used to be a stripper.

I had been thinking that my relationship with Charles would bring me closer to having a 'normal' life of love, trust and companionship. A pregnancy was never intended, at least not by me, as it stood in the way of my finding more secure employment, and just having fun with a caring guy. And so I told him that if he didn't have plans for this baby, I wanted an abortion.

'Of course, I have plans!' he exclaimed. 'I plan to be a daddy!'
And I believed him.

There was something funny about that time at Harry's Pancakes. All the women – everyone from the manager to my co-workers – were falling pregnant. Someone joked that there was something special in the pancakes! And maybe there was, because a mutual bond developed between all of us, and it made the time I spent at work more comfortable.

And I needed it, because away from work, during that first trimester, things were hell.

I couldn't find Charles. When I did, he was playing this cool guy all over the clubs. During those first four months, during the very few times we were together at his place, Charles verbally abused me, and would kick me and beat me up when I asked him why he was suddenly behaving this way. But he continued to say he wanted to be a daddy to the baby.

At first my mother was also excited about the baby, because now the community around her could see the fruits of the 'African way'. She was dancing about having a baby in her family. But then she too became verbally abusive again, and we continued arguing a lot. Even so, I kept coming back to her when Charles gave me problems.

So I was very grumpy during my pregnancy. I was also very worried when I had to have a blood test. I calmed myself by saying at least I had God at my side. At four-and-a-half months pregnant, an HIV check at Somerset Hospital came up negative for me, and I was relieved.

But things with Charles had not improved. He went quiet for several weeks, and after five or six months of pregnancy I gave up and started to ignore him back.

When Charles then beat me up again during my pregnancy, I decided no, this wasn't going to work. This was the type of abuse I was running away from. I moved away from his place and moved in with my mom.

I just focused on the baby growing inside me and towards the end of the pregnancy I started really enjoying it. I saved my money and provided food for the house, which made my mother happy. I had worked throughout the nine months, which also shocked her, but she was pleased. And I enjoyed having my co-workers help me prepare for the birth.

Charles signed the Home Affairs papers for the baby's birth certificate and got his ID immediately. I eventually figured it out that he had wanted a baby so he could get South African citizenship.

I was high on weed the day I first felt my contractions. It was around three in the afternoon. But the contractions continued for a long time, and the weed wore off. In the hospital, I pushed and pushed, and enjoyed the morphine, which numbed me.

My son S was born at Cape Town's Somerset Hospital on Heritage Day – just after midnight on 24 September 2008.

It was a difficult birth, and the hospital was full, so just a few hours after S was born, I had to return to my mom's house.

When I arrived home, there were these village women waiting to welcome me and the baby. These grannies were sitting in the dining room, drinking *umqomboti*, sniffing snuff, and as I walked in they started ululating '*Umzukulwana*'.

In Xhosa culture, there are very strict rules about the birth of a baby. A baby must not be seen by strangers until the aunties have welcomed the baby. But while my mother was receiving praise from the community grannies, I was thinking, 'Hell no, these township grannies ain't going to touch *my* baby!'

I was exhausted and I needed to sleep. So I just looked at them, and then I left them and went into the room I was sharing with my mom, to sleep on my mattress on the floor.

My mother had at least tried to make things pleasant by getting the room ready for the baby. The heater was on, and the room was nice and warm. Behind me I heard one granny say, 'Well, we grew up in the village, and the village is *never* quiet until after midday. First thing we hear is a chicken, and the rest is all of us walking and talking loud. We are here now, so she must get over it.'

There was something important that happened after S was born, even if I found all the cultural stuff irritating. It was that this was when my mother started calling me '*ntombi*' (my daughter). The baby had brought her cultural integrity because she was now a grandmother. And gradually, in the eyes of the Khayelitsha community, my mother became less like an 'auntie' and more like a mother to me.

It was also, however, the start of many arguments and disputes about culture and religion between us.

Following Christian methods, I took S to be circumcised after seven days. This shocked my mother and her community grannies.

'You never taught me culture,' I said to my mom. 'You were never in my life to teach me that. How can you tell me at my age now that I must respect your culture?' I explained that I was committed to Christianity, and that that was my background, not this Xhosa culture she was always trying to rub in.

I also knew that most of what my mother had learnt about Xhosa culture came from her late husband, Richard. So I continued, 'I'm not going to respect your husband who I hardly even knew!'

My mother would then launch into a long story telling me all that her husband did for her and her family. Bitterly, I remembered that, as a nine-year-old, I was not considered her child but her brother's child. I had never been included in this family she now spoke of with such respect.

But the cultural pressures continued.

After S had had his immunisations, I came home one day and noticed a smell about him. Then I noticed the red wool tied around his waist, which in Xhosa culture is supposed to drive away the evil forces. I was furious! My mother said she had called a neighbour to make S '*ukukhupha umoya*'.

I cut off the wool and shoved it in the bin.

'If you don't believe this culture, your son will be confused,' she yelled at me.

I just replied, 'No!'

After S was circumcised, I took him home and faced a smug mom, who said, 'You see, you think you know everything. It's going to bite you, just you wait!'

It was very difficult to deal with all this. I was struggling to feed the baby as well – I was told my breasts were too large to nurse him as I would suffocate him, so I had to bottle feed him with special milk, which cost R120 a week. My mother and I had arguments over that too.

I had tried to get together with Charles to ask for his support and explore how we could live together as a family. Instead of discussing it, he'd shouted at me. He stayed around in Khayelitsha long enough to see the baby born, but then he left.

After S was born, I returned to work at Harry's Pancakes. I

was trying to be a good mother for the first time, trying to care for the baby while working, trying to save money responsibly. I needed my mom's assistance. But things weren't easy between us and I felt there was a lot of pressure.

I paid her R500 every month to look after S while I went out to work, and I still had to pay for his expensive milk. Sometimes I wondered if she really deserved to carry the title of 'grandmother', and not 'babysitter', as if we shared a contract rather than blood.

And I was exhausted from it all. At night in our one room where my mom, S and I slept on the floor, S would wake up and cry. If I continued sleeping, my mother would yell at me.

But even with all this going on in those first few months, I just loved this baby. I would spend ages just looking at him; bathing him was always a time filled with precious bonding moments.

When Z was born, I had only seen him for a few seconds – I'd just had a flashing image of his big eyes and curly hair. With S it was the same image, but I could now stare at him for hours, drinking in the sight of him. I loved his tiny baby hands, and I appreciated him every single day.

I had always carried this feeling of loss for Z. This new baby brought love into my heart for the first time; I knew I had to be my best for him, because he had trusted me with his life – now there was this tiny baby, and it was him I had to learn to care for. It was a responsibility that removed me from my own self-interest, because my whole life I had been concerned about my own survival and protection.

S made me feel that I have survived, even though I wasn't yet ready to be the person I knew I needed to be for him. I made promises in my heart for him: 'Please, S, give me time. I promise you things will change.'

I would say this to him every day.

My mother still had her business of selling beer to support everyone in the house – my two step brothers plus now S. She was drinking a lot and selling wine. We had so many arguments about money, which made me very tired.

Then Harry's Pancakes closed down and I lost my job. Mom's noise in my ears got louder and louder.

'You've got to support yourself. And what about me? And S?' she would repeat.

During our arguments, my ears, heart and body would be shaking. I think my little baby felt and heard my anxiety and my increasing anger.

Weed helped me shut out her noise, so I smoked more and more, but it was clear that I couldn't live with my mother any more. And I knew I had to make money so that I could afford a separate home for my son and myself. I would not allow him to grow up with the abusive parent that I had had.

I just wished I could be alone with S in a quiet place.

I was twenty-eight years old. S was two months old. His father was gone. And through all the noise I had this spiritual feeling that was growing. I wanted things to be right.

Twenty-two

FOR THE PERIODS THAT WE were together, my mother and I had argued a lot and I had always felt we needed something to bond us together. The answer was S. He was her baby too. Despite all the arguments, I was strengthened by having my mother near me because most of the time I had no idea what to do with this baby. She helped me care for him, and I think it was the first time we had something we shared.

I decided I needed to continue the spiritual journey I had started with the Methodists in Johannesburg. I also needed to find an income. I knew one hundred per cent that I would return to S, and that I wasn't going to repeat what my mother had done to me. That wasn't going to happen. But to make a new path in my life, I knew I had to get away from my mom.

That December 2008, just a few months after S's birth, I left for Johannesburg to find a job. My mother wanted me to return to prostitution. That, to her, was my job. She didn't seem to realise how much I didn't want to go back to that lifestyle.

I knew I had to get away, and then come back stronger.

And it came at a great cost: I left parenting S in order to resurrect my spirit.

In the back of my mind, I thought I would stay in Yeoville with Lindiwe, my pretty Cape Town friend. She knew my story – knew about the working and occasional stripping in Cape Town, knew about me getting pregnant and having S. She thought that I was in Johannesburg to look for clients and continue my prostitution business now that I had a bigger family to support.

When I arrived in Johannesburg, Lindiwe immediately fixed me up to perform on a bachelor's party strip show which she had organised for her friend's fiancé.

The money was tempting – R1200, a good amount for a night's work. The party was inside a big bus with a bar inside and a pole for me to dance and strip on, and it drove from one club to the next while the guys watched me strip. The guys kept buying me drinks, and I was high on weed.

So that was how I started things back in Joburg.

When I was staying with Lindiwe, she kept going out, and that's when I learnt that she was now also attending functions at the Methodist church. When she found out I was also joining the Methodists, she became very embarrassed because she had introduced me to this strip bus, not knowing about my spiritual pursuits.

Then Lindiwe found out that the soup kitchen staff and others in the church already knew me and my background from the last time I'd been there. I thought to myself, 'This chick could threaten me.'

And she was about to do just that – Lindiwe was about to make my life hell.

Once I had made contact with the Methodist church, I moved out of Lindiwe's place and into the Methodists' Home of Hope shelter. While I was there, I learnt about a six-month programme designed to guide 'young' women like myself, who were having difficulties with life in general, in the direction of the Christian faith. It was called IntombiMayano. When I joined up, it was like I was 'on trial', trying to become a spiritually strong young woman and forget my years of trauma.

Lindiwe, whom I had considered a close friend, didn't seem to understand the spiritual changes I was experiencing, and that I preferred to continue with church activities rather than prostitution. Nor was she accepting of my spiritual growth, even though we went through the programme together. And while I was so excited to come back to the Methodists, Lindiwe seemed uncomfortable with my move, perhaps because I might crowd her own space there. That's where we had our differences.

She might have been willing to help support me, but the church was full of TV celebrities, and she felt I wasn't fitting into this image. By now, Lindiwe was an extra on a local TV show, and was moving about with the 'celebrities'. With everyone knowing my story, I felt like I was living in a fish bowl.

I challenged her: 'You're an actress now. So why are you also joining this church programme?'

The dynamics between us started to change.

The IntombiMayano programme enabled me to not only learn religious and Godly principles for conducting my life, but also to make friends within the church, and give service by working in their soup kitchen. During that time we could only wear our black and white clothes.

But at the same time, my mother had been phoning me from Cape Town to complain about money, and she was making me feel so small and cheap. When I spoke to S on the phone, I would reassure him that I was his mama and would be coming home soon. But as I neared the end of the six months, I became totally focused on my spiritual path, even forgetting about my mother and S, and the anxiety I had been feeling about them.

I ignored my mom's voice more and more, and instead I focused on helping the kids in the church's orphanages. And I was able to stay in the Home of Hope shelter, which helped my focus. By now I was making choices that were free from the violent and abusive circumstances of the past. I had found a church community which supported my growth, and it felt like my time had finally arrived. When I completed my six months, I received a uniform that identified me as an *intombimayano*.

Right after receiving my Methodist uniform, I had the opportunity to visit Cape Town and see my mother and S in Site C. The grannies in Site C also wear their 'cultural' garbs for church, so I impressed them by wearing my garb that Sunday. I really felt that I was getting somewhere. I went back to Joburg feeling good about things.

Then, a shock.

Just when I had my full uniform and had found a stronger

spiritual path, my friendship with Lindiwe fell apart. One day, we were both called into the church office and told that rumours were spreading among the members. Lindiwe stated in that meeting that I had told her that the church pastor was a client of mine from when I was a sex worker. Her own circle of friends had been spreading this rumour as well.

I said in that meeting, with the pastor present, 'I never met this pastor in my previous life.'

The pastor stood up and agreed with me: 'This is not true, this rumour. I have never had any relations of a sexual nature with Grizelda!' And then he surprised me by saying: 'This rumour is very hurtful and I'm afraid Grizelda will have to leave my church. I cannot have my name muddied like this. My position in this church is more important than her past.'

The church leaders said I must leave the congregation and not work at the soup kitchen any more. This rejection hurt me profoundly. I left, and never saw Lindiwe or discussed this false rumour with her after that.

The rejection from the church and betrayal from someone I had thought was my best friend plunged me once again into deep depression.

Just as I had chosen the path of survival, I was being set back once again. I asked God why I deserved that, just when I thought I was doing the right thing.

One lady in the church said I could continue working on Saturdays at the soup kitchen. I was very confused. I disliked the shelter's 'sorry-shame' programme, which meant begging and looking poor for the white people who came with their donations and gave us food. That didn't allow for spiritual growth.

I also didn't know if I would be allowed to go back to the Home of Hope shelter, or if I had to stay on the street. I started looking at other shelters and programmes to join. The Home of Hope shelter allowed me to stay, although they weren't happy that I was spending time on other church programmes.

Then I was invited by a church member to stay in her apartment in Joburg central until I found my feet. Her apartment had three bedrooms, and she lived there with her boyfriend, two children, and her sister, Zanele.

I think the woman was worried that her boyfriend would want to have sex with me, because she made me sleep on the balcony. Although I was grateful for the bed, in my mind I queried whether she really trusted me. I found it unsettling that she was so suspicious of me. I just couldn't understand why someone from the church would try to help me, but then not trust me in their home. On the streets I had been called useless and unreliable, and I hadn't expected the same treatment now, when I was trying to change for the better. I left after a month, but in that time I had developed a close friendship with her sister, Zanele.

After that I wandered about, and would find odd jobs for income, like washing people's clothes. One time a guy tried to approach me for favours, but I just got very angry. I was not interested in engaging with any men.

I had to find my own feet again. I was deeply hurt and confused. Yet, I had to make some money for myself, S and my mother in Cape Town. My mother was drinking and still expected me to prostitute myself for income. We had a toxic relationship, even from this distance.

A Zulu guy I knew in the church referred me to a Pakistani

guy who owned a tuck shop in Soweto, and that's how in my vulnerable condition I was trafficked by a church member: I could work and live in this man's house, but I had to give sex for my accommodation.

My spiritual growth had cleansed me, but my progress was being challenged by the devil, who kept pulling me towards temptation. I still needed to earn money, and I knew I could do it with sex, but at the same time I wanted to be left alone!

I spoke with God: 'Please, don't let me down. Don't let me down.'

Twenty-three

GOD, IN THE END, DID not give me the money, but after a week He helped me to get out of Soweto and back to my friend Zanele.

Zanele was still attending the Houghton Methodist Church, but she introduced me to Tie, a Zimbabwean girl, who suggested I join her Christ Embassy Church in Yeoville. I kept strong, kept the faith, and considered joining the CEC community.

In the meantime, friends I made led me to others who helped me find jobs, like domestic work. My employers were caring when they didn't know my background. Sometimes, maybe once a month, I would still go to bachelor parties and do strip shows.

When I eventually joined the Christ Embassy Church, I discovered that the Nigerian pastor was very charismatic, encouraging rigid practices of fasting during the week, preaching the gospel and holding conferences. The programme promoted forgiveness and prosperity in life, and this helped my spiritual path further. I felt that my spiritual strength was paying off; I could grow in this new church.

But I was still being pulled back to work at the Methodist soup kitchen. I felt good about my walk from Hillbrow to Houghton at 5am to cook rice and chicken for people who were on the streets, like I once was. I could also receive a day's meal for myself, and this kept my spirits up. It was as though I was overcoming, even forgiving, my former church for abandoning me, and allowing me to still exercise my spiritual and civic duties towards others in need, against all odds. I saw the change my work was making in the lives of other people.

But it was painful for me – being torn between two churches. I loved the Methodist church for what I learnt from it, but in the end I was experiencing more growth at Christ Embassy.

After two-and-a-half years, I finally stopped working in the Methodist soup kitchen because I developed a runny tummy! It seemed to me then that my system was being purged of stress and confusion.

And what was I to do with the uniform I had earned with the Methodists who cast me out? Thinking about it all over again made me very angry, so much so that I threw the uniform into a street bin.

A woman who was watching me told me that God would curse me for that. 'You can't just change churches like that,' she said.

Yet Christ Embassy, which was more charismatic and emotion-driven, inspired me to grow. And I was happy at least that the Methodists had taught me discipline during a time when I needed to get off drugs and prostitution.

Yes, now I was making choices, like I couldn't have during my time of being trafficked. I was evolving.

But old thoughts plagued me as I continued to walk my spiritual path. I knew how to find money – with clients. I also knew the trade-off: sex workers always needed their fix. I remembered how one girl I knew had drunk Benylin cough syrup and then smoked cigarettes just to stay high.

Should I go back to this kind of life, even temporarily?

I had other thoughts: had I *enjoyed* sex during my prostitution days? No. I had always worried about satisfying the client so that he would return. I had never thought about satisfying myself. Yes, I would like to have a loving relationship with someone who could physically satisfy me. In my life, I had only climaxed during a threesome with another girl.

Most importantly, I had to make some decisions about money, and my choices were muddled by the economic realities of my situation: I was undereducated, underskilled for employment, and I still needed to get off the sex and the hard drugs. Those addictions were still calling me.

My mom's phone calls angered me. She was always asking for money, saying things like, 'You have a child.' In my phone calls to my mom, I always tried to reassure her that I would send more money. But it wasn't happening.

I desperately looked in other directions.

Twenty-four

I SOMETIMES WONDER WHY I have so often been at the wrong place at the wrong time. Something else happened during these Joburg years that later really made me question what was going on in my life.

I was still going through what I thought was my spiritual transformation, and meeting lots of people at the Nigerian Christ Embassy Church. I became aware that there were other activities going on at the church – some people who I had seen at church conferences were also involved in less spiritual business. I really wanted to change, so it was a challenge to accept what was going on, but I just washed it off.

When I found myself still struggling with life, I went with the flow. And backslid again.

A girlfriend of mine, Portia, had got to know some top Nigerians in the church. They flew us both to Cape Town for a big celebration – they had booked out an entire hotel in Tableview. I was happy about this opportunity because it gave me a chance to visit my little son and my mom.

Once we were there, I was surprised to discover how deeply Portia was involved. She kept her BMW at her home in Cape Town, and together we drove to Tableview.

On the way, we stopped at a garage to fill up with petrol.

In the car, as we were putting on our make-up, a white guy waved to us.

'Jeez, Cape Town has got so friendly!' I exclaimed to Portia.

Then he came over to us from his little red Golf. He seemed middle-aged, almost bald, with his little patch of grass swept to one side. I could hear that he wasn't South African but British. We chatted bit.

'Will you go on a date with me?' he suddenly asked me.

'That sounds very personal,' I said.

'Yeah,' he returned, 'but you look like a very beautiful South African girl.'

I was all excited at having a British guy trying to pick me up! I looked into his green eyes, and politely told him that we had a function to hurry to. He gave me his card and we exchanged numbers before saying goodbye.

Portia and I then drove to the hotel. I had never seen a bunch of black guys take over a hotel before, but these guys had real money. I learnt that the drug lords were celebrating several years of successful moneymaking by having one huge party. What was funny for me was that I knew some of the small guys who were standing around selling their stuff.

I also knew that I was there to work, though. So I asked Portia who my client was in this gathering.

'It's the main guy!' she replied. 'He's into girls with big boobs!' Portia herself had a bum but small boobs. That's how I discovered that a tall Nigerian guy called King had booked me for the whole week.

When I met him a bit later, I carefully asked for my R12 000 upfront, which he gave me. For that amount of money, I assumed I was booked to entertain not only King but other men as well.

King gave me my own room, but he wasn't around much and when he did visit my room he would just sleep. King had apparently booked me to be the pretty lady with the tall clicking heels who he could show off at the events. But I wasn't sleeping with him.

I got bored. I'd been out to have lots of fun that weekend, so I ended up shagging King's friend Jay instead, just for fun. Jay even gave me his bank card, which provided a good laugh for Portia and myself, although I wasn't going to play around with it in case he went crazy.

King found out I had sex with his friend, but he didn't scold me. He just wasn't happy about it. He ended up sending me to Jay. And then Jay also disappeared.

Now I didn't have my own client and I became really bored hanging out in this hotel with nothing to do. I was used to the fast pace of Joburg, and this week in Cape Town was moving so slowly. I was also disappointed because I'd been looking forward to having fun, partying and getting drunk. After all, I had been flown down especially for this week's events, but now nothing was happening.

So, I called the British guy, whose number I still had with me.

'Hey, how are you? You alright?' he answered.

We chatted, and then arranged for him to come to the hotel for a drink.

Sitting at the bar, at first this guy seemed quite interesting. I had always enjoyed meeting intelligent men who talked about interesting things before we moved towards the sex. That is how I had learnt a lot about life – from men who took the time to show me that respect. But then it seemed to me that this guy was obsessed with race.

When he drank his first drink, I got the feeling he was forcing himself to get drunk because he knew he was going to shag a black lady.

During his second drink, I heard, 'African girls are hot, sexy; but South African girls are ... like ... crooks.' His voice became hard.

He got to his third drink and, slurring, made more derogatory remarks about 'South African girls'. By now, I was picking up his anger and hatred. I wondered if he was a freak, like a serial killer. I gave him the benefit of the doubt. He saw that I wasn't pleased with the conversation and he perked up.

'Oh, I'm sure you're very different from the other black girls I've met.'

By the time we got to his place, a flat in Century City, he was very drunk. We talked and then had sex, but I felt so uncomfortable. He was mumbling about how he wanted to slap and beat a 'black bitch' – everything he said was racist and abusive.

I hadn't thought of him as a client but as a 'date' – and this was no fantasy date. Things were going very wrong.

Why am I doing this? I asked myself, and came to my senses.

I got him off me. I went to the toilet, with my phone. Inside, I called my friend Portia, telling her where I was and to come get me, fast.

Then came my Oscar Pistorius moment.

The guy smashed the toilet door with an axe!

I saw the axe coming through the door, and I screamed.

On the phone, Portia could hear what was going on, and I was screaming and shouting, 'Portia, come get me. This guy has an axe! I'm naked!'

He continued axing the door.

'Who the fuck are you calling?' he yelled at me. 'Open this door!' He was swearing, 'you black bitch' and the 'k' word.

He got the door open just as his flat mate walked into the room: 'What's going on?'

Then both of them grabbed me by the hair, and start beating me up and kicking me.

Moments later, Security arrived, having heard me screaming. Portia and a Nigerian guy arrived then too, while I was being punched outside the toilet, stark naked. I didn't know this Nigerian, but seeing a white guy beating up a black girl made him crazy. He grabbed the man and beat him senseless.

'We don't do that in Cape Town!' he yelled.

Then the police arrived, having been called by Security.

I opened a police case against this British guy, who the police locked up.

To the police I stated that I didn't know these people who had beat him up, that he'd got beaten for his own reasons. His defence was that he was using the axe because he thought I was calling people to rob him.

I returned to Joburg and the court proceedings didn't happen for several months. At first he begged me not to open a case against him. When I opened a case anyway, he kept calling me, asking me to drop the case.

I returned to Cape Town for the court proceedings. There, a former victim of his, a white girl now in a wheelchair, testified that he had beaten her up so badly that she was now paralysed. She had made a case against him then, but the police hadn't been able to catch him until my case was opened. What a freak.

He was indicted, locked up for several years, then deported and banned from entering South Africa again.

Later, my friends asked why I had ever phoned this British guy, a total stranger. And I don't know why I called him, except that I wanted to be with a man, to have sex, to have fun. And once again I was high on drugs.

This is the disaster of addiction.

Twenty-five

IN JOBURG OVER THE NEXT few years, I continued my spiritual quest. It was always the same: when there was stability in my life I could get off drugs, but I was pushed back when things went wrong.

I still needed a more permanent home, despite the kindness of my friends Zanele and Tie. Zanele found me a room to rent from a Congolese woman for R400 a month. But I had to sleep on the floor in the kitchen, with no mattress.

'Salvation is personal,' I said to myself.

Zanele and I continued to attend the Christ Embassy Church.

I was still wanting spiritual upliftment to help me escape from my memories of abuse and sexual violence. The CEC had become my place for developing faith, strength and friendships.

I decided to get off heavy drugs, which wasn't easy. The first year was tough, and I just smoked weed, but I felt clean and good about myself.

I started a new job as a nanny, looking after the grandchild of one of the women from the Methodist church. By then my need for drugs had diminished; I knew I couldn't smell of drugs and be a good worker, knew I couldn't always be thinking of how to steal and get the next drug fix.

This woman's other daughter, Nuro, attended CEC with me, and her mother suggested we both leave 'that Nigerian church'. It caused some friction between Nuro and her mother. But at least I had a steady job, and I was on a good path by then.

Nuro became a significant part of my life and transformation. She and I spent a lot of time speaking about the Bible. I also shared my trafficking stories with her, which fascinated her. I was getting used to stability, having work and friends around while going to church and gradually leading a more sober and simple life. It was nice. I was getting stronger and stronger.

Then, another setback. My landlord suddenly doubled my rent to R800. This was unaffordable since I was receiving a nanny's salary of R2200, and I felt it was unfair since I was sleeping on the kitchen floor! Drama broke out in the church about this so I gave up the accommodation, but to add insult to injury, I was fired as a nanny because Nuro's mother did not approve of us attending the Christ Embassy Church. A woman in the CEC found me a job as a cleaner, which paid slightly more than my salary as a nanny, although that didn't last long.

Tie came to the rescue by letting me share her bed in a bachelor flat for R400. Her flat was right behind a drug house.

My transformation was never simple. Because of the world I knew, the skills I had and the demands of my life, I always had to make difficult decisions.

The house behind Nuro's flat was run by Nigerians. Delivering their drugs to Cape Town was an easy way of making money. I was no longer taking heavy drugs myself, so it wasn't a big issue for me to pick up and deliver them, and not consume them myself.

Hearing my mother was sick in hospital, I managed to make a drug drop in Cape Town, gather a few thousand rand, see my mother and my son and then leave again for Joburg.

I had street protection for these money stashes I carried around. I carried all my money in my bra and in my shoe as I didn't have a bank account. Gangsters on the streets have a secret language and invisible bonds, so they leave you alone. I was not robbed because there was always a network of people keeping an eye on me. And I knew I was already part of the drug dealers' safety network – they knew I was reliable.

Sometimes, I did not accept an opportunity for dropping drugs as I was always wanting to phase down this activity. But mostly they would offer me this money – R11 000, R12 000 – and the sound of those numbers in my desperate ears would draw me in.

Then, when I came back from a delivery, my body would go into shock, and I would run straight to the church and cry for mercy! That's what I found myself doing: I did what I did to support my family, hoping that when I was done, God would bless and forgive me.

My spiritual meter kept swinging back and forth as I entertained these thoughts in my head.

Twenty-six

DURING MY VARIOUS EXPLOITS IN Joburg, I became attached to four men who paid me well each month to 'keep' me for periods of time. One of these men was Suleiman, a businessman who was gentle and sweet with me. Originally from Tanzania, he lived in Cape Town.

I enjoyed his company, and got to know him well. I never let him know about my past; I lied about my life and background. I just told him I was in Joburg 'doing my thing' as a waitress. I thought that if he knew about me, it would spoil the type of relationship I was hoping might develop with him.

When we were apart Suleiman liked phone sex, but he would sometimes travel to be with me for a few days in Joburg. He also paid me to visit him in Cape Town, and I would manage to secretly and briefly visit my son and mom. In Joburg or in Cape Town, I would stay with him for several days at a time.

He never told me what business he was into, but he paid me well, which gave him authority over me. Sometimes I thought I was becoming emotionally attached to him, and he seemed interested in me too, because he was caring and loving.

But he also became very controlling.

I couldn't take any drugs in front of him, because he disapproved. Rather, I would have to sneak them into my system before we met up so I would be high during our time together. He didn't like me smoking weed either, so it was a whole mission to try to camouflage my weed as a cigarettes, and then I'd gargle with mouthwash to kill the smell.

If I came to his house in Cape Town, he wouldn't let me leave. And if I needed to go out, like shopping for something, I had to give him a very good reason. He locked me in the house when he went out. My phone always had to be on because he would frequently call me.

Because I was also doing drug drops, I had two SIM cards for my phone. So if we went out, say to the mall, I'd make sure I had both SIM cards with me. I sometimes needed to call my drug lord to deliver the drugs, so once at the mall, I would excuse myself from Suleiman and go to the ladies' toilets to change my SIM and call my pimp. Then I'd switch back to the only number Suleiman had for me.

I also always had to find ways of keeping myself high in order to service his needs, so while I was in the toilets, I'd quickly smoke some weed with cigarette tobacco. Then I'd meet up with him somewhere where there were lots of people – hoping he wouldn't focus on my body and smell.

Sometimes Suleiman called me during one of my SIM-card swops, and got my voice message. When he asked me why I had turned off my phone, I had to tell him I dropped it, or got water inside it, or something. Then he would angrily ask who I'd really been calling.

I had to do what he wanted me to, when he wanted it.

Sometimes, I thought he was crazy. He would make me stand naked in front of him to check my body and my bum, to make sure I smelt good. If I didn't smell right, he would ask me to take another shower. He followed Muslim sanitation rules and demanded cleanliness at all times. I had to wear long dresses inside the house, and cover my whole body. This made me crazy, wearing so many clothes.

But he was paying me well, so I didn't want to mess things up. And I was still fond of him because he could be really romantic. Sulieman would sometimes do nothing with me sexually – we would just lie together, or talk. Or he would sit up in bed with the light on and look at my nude body. Or he would decorate the whole house with candles while I just lay there. We wouldn't have intercourse but would just watch each other play with ourselves.

When we did have sex, he thought he was the greatest performer. I felt sorry for him, because he wasn't particularly satisfying, but I just let him do whatever he wanted to do. And because I liked him, I gave him more pleasure. I didn't tell him I was getting emotionally attached, and I always took my morning-after tablet.

One night in Cape Town, Suleiman asked not to use a condom, and when I returned to Joburg after that, he became very quiet. He owed me R6000 for those few days' visit with him, but his money hadn't been transferred into my re-opened bank account.

I called him: 'When are you sending my money?'

He dropped the phone, and this happened several more times.

When he finally called me, giving excuses about difficulties with his business, I told him to consider the baby I was carrying.

Of course I was lying, but he freaked out.

But what did he expect? I thought. I had cooperated with him by having sex without a condom. His side of the deal was that he had to pay me.

When we'd first met, I had thought he was single, but by now I had found out that he had a wife who lived somewhere outside Cape Town. So I sent him threatening SMSes telling him that I knew everything about him, as well as his mother's address and his wife's address.

I said, 'I'm going to call them right now and tell them who I am and that I know where you stay in Cape Town, and what you're on about.'

We went on back and forth. I gave him a sob story, telling him that I really wanted to keep this baby because I felt something had developed between us.

'I feel this can work with us,' I said.

'What will my parents in Tanzania think if I told them?' On and on, he told me all his challenges: 'My wife cannot have this trauma right now – she has her own traumas.'

I retorted, 'I have nothing to do with your problems. What about me and my kid?'

He asked me to get rid of the baby, saying we would have a longer relationship without the complication. Then he sent me money each week for an abortion. He asked if he could get me a place to stay in Cape Town so that we could be closer together.

'No,' I said. 'This is happening now, this baby. And I want it.' I wasn't going to go anywhere.

I never really cared what happened when I told stories like these. I would never worry about the outcome. I would always justify it to myself, because there was always something I needed – a drug, a client, money – to survive.

Suleiman really started to freak out. When he cried over the phone, I felt quite stupid about telling my lie. But I went on.

I asked him to come to Joburg to be with me for the abortion. He said he couldn't. I insisted that if I had an abortion, I wanted him there with me, otherwise I would not do it.

I said, 'I've always been a support to you, so why can't you support me now?'

And that's when he turned on me. 'What? Now you're sounding like a girlfriend. Since when did you become emotional?'

I was now sure that all men are the same. The same issues.

He said he would send money to me via a friend. But I rejected that idea. What if the friend killed me or did something violent to me to make me lose the baby? Then he agreed to send me R4000 before the abortion, and R4000 afterwards, as long as I sent a form from the clinic confirming that the procedure had been done.

I continued to insist he be in Joburg with me during the abortion. If he had actually flown to see me in Joburg, I would have told him I wasn't pregnant. I would have told him the truth. And the truth was that I just wanted to see him because

I liked him.

Eventually I realised that I couldn't convince him, so I had to settle with accepting money and not communicating any longer.

Was I going to continue looking for a loving, caring relationship after that?

Twenty-seven

If there wasn't romance, at least there was friendship.

When I was in my early thirties, two friends from church, Nuro and Lesedi, came to understand and support me in different ways. These two women gave me the company I had always needed: they were there for me. I felt their understanding. Lesedi would buy me food when I didn't have any money, and Nuro was always finding me information about work that was available at the church. Nuro knew my story and just wanted to help me to be strong and become 'delivered' in the church.

As time went on, I tried to return the favour. Looking back,

I told her how someone holds your head during the blow job so you can't get away. I told her how I experienced forced blow jobs, and how I had to take four ecstasy tablets and half a bottle of Jack Daniels in order to deal with it. I told her how the skin of your mouth is broken, how your head is pulled back, how sometimes you are whipped while it's happening. I showed her the pimples on my gums, and how discoloured my teeth were.

I told her it's not an exciting, arousing, butterfly feeling. That there are better ways to be a super-strong woman.

Nuro had had her own experiences of sexual exploitation in her job as an usher at the church.

I asked her, 'Why are you still ushering if you're getting exploited?'

'But I don't know where to go,' she said.

'Now you know how I felt!'

I enjoyed seeing Nuro respond to this wake-up call.

In the end it was the church itself that released me from the cycle I was in.

I got a voluntary job at the Christ Embassy Church call centre in Randburg, where I had lots of contacts through Lesedi. People phoned the call centre about their physical ailments; on behalf of the church, I had to take the calls and say prayers for each caller. I had been led to believe by the church that if I attended a four-day conference and volunteered in the call centre, I would be eligible for a salaried job.

When I approached management about getting a paid job, they said they couldn't pay me because I 'needed to grow spiritually'. In a call centre, you need to grow spiritually? And they thought I didn't have enough spiritual experience to be of service to others? If nothing else, as a volunteer in the call

Thoughts about my future caused me so much anxiety, even though I knew I needed to change and find my purpose. As I exited from the horrors and dislocations of my past life of prostitution, drugs and other abuses, what would I have to face next?

At the age of thirty-two, in 2013, I decided to avoid temptation by returning to Cape Town permanently.

I returned to my mother and S five years after I left them. I arrived with some income saved up, but more importantly, I came with a change in spirit, an upliftment, a maturity and growth towards sobriety and even some semblance of inner happiness.

I had learnt not to turn my anger on others or to blame them for what had happened to me. Rather, it was *my* life, and in that life, I was responsible for caring for my son. I would not allow my anger to focus on him, like my mom's anger had throughout my life.

Once I was home, I looked at the city of my childhood. I was impressed with the way the Democratic Alliance was cleaning up Cape Town – I didn't see as many street kids as there were when I was young. I thought that the DA was reputable, and so I got a job working in their call centre. And I became one of two-hundred-and-fifty coloureds and Africans, speaking several indigenous languages, engaged in heated political debate.

With the DA job I earned a decent income and learnt more about the racial realities in my society. Working there made me realise that I could change professions and hold a job developing awareness. This job empowered me to understand the world better, to work hard, to gain skills and to feel I was doing a worthwhile and useful service.

In my childhood, I had known only a little about Mandela

and the ANC Youth League. Now, I was becoming more politicised, and realising the importance of activism. The DA job prompted me to begin working in public awareness.

I then saw a request on Facebook for anyone who had experienced sexual exploitation and abuse. I responded and told my story, which was filmed for a programme on SABC 2. This opened up even more speaking events. I just continued to pray to God to keep providing these opportunities. My newfound spiritual strength helped me develop confidence to talk publicly about the gender issues so close to my heart.

I became excited knowing that my vision and purpose was to write and talk about the horrors of sex trafficking. Working with the Embrace Dignity NGO allowed me to do this.

This, I knew, was the work I was cut out to do.

It has not always been easy. At times, my physical, emotional and financial needs have overwhelmed me to a point of wondering if I can ever realise my vision.

I have also had to deal with the stigma of the strip club community who know my past. When I came back to Cape Town permanently, I had enough money that I didn't need to find clients. But I would still go to the clubs – maybe just out of habit. The bouncer would say, 'Hey, welcome back! You just missed out at the big convention event ...' And there it was: this assumption about who I was and what I wanted.

Habits are hard to change. The minute he reminded me of my old life, my mind would jump wildly: 'Let me find a client for tonight.'

I didn't though. I just watched. I would see how the regular folks who came in were familiar with the girls, recommending them to each other. It is so hard to step out once you are in these circles. You become part of a network.

There were other things I had to face too.

I needed to seriously look at matters of health. As a survivor for the past few years, I am only now going through the emotional process of caring for myself. And nothing is simple. Because I had headaches, I went to an eye doctor. At the appointment, I hated him testing my eyes – my vision got very blurry and I couldn't see. I was very scared, and I started crying. Confused, the doctor asked me why I was crying.

I explained: 'When you look into my eyes, it reminds me of the masking tape I had to wear over my eyes during my Joburg bondage.'

I am still healing, and wounds hurt as they heal.

As a survivor, I want to grow as fast as I can, learn how society works, what it does, and how I can 'fit in' and be independent.

I'm learning to manage my story. When I talk publicly, I feel like I am undressing myself. I'm always wondering what other people are thinking of me. This paranoia will pass, I hope.

It is still hard for me to be a single black girl in an African community, especially since I have a son to raise. It's hard for me to get involved in emotional relationships, to tell a guy my background. I keep wondering, 'When is he coming to me?' I have never had any stable trusting loving relationship that didn't disappoint me.

Also, I am only now facing this process of reconciliation with my mother, having her confront the reality that she abandoned me. This pain hurts us both, but we are working through it, and growing trust between us.

I have always been perplexed about why my mother and my

dad gave up on me in my childhood years and never included me when they started their own families elsewhere. Was I not 'family'?

When my mother lived and worked at the docks, I thought she didn't care about me. But now that we are talking, she tells me: 'You know what? I don't even know if they told you at the shelter that I used to bring clothes and other stuff for you.' And I think it's true, looking back, that my mother provided some things for me, maybe even further back, when I was living in Woodstock.

I understand my mother better now too. She is also going through change, meeting her own challenges. Her bouts of drinking have made it difficult for me to reconcile with her, and it has sometimes worn me down. We're still adjusting, but the peaceful times we have together are a blessing, and we are working on it.

Sometimes my mother says the prayers that I have taught her. She sometimes asks me to help her with certain scriptures. I think my journey is rubbing off on her. She is learning, and now it's in her life. I am proud to say that I have changed, and now she is changing too.

I have learnt from S the importance of loving and how to extend that love. Now that I am present, at home, he can identify me as his mom. There's some normality to our lives now; we're like a typical family, with Granny caring for him as I work. This makes life and loving easier.

S is the voice that keeps me going. When he calls me 'Mama', it is my strength.

Author's note

WHAT DO I TELL PEOPLE who ask me who I am?

I say I'm a recovered drug addict.

What drove me to drugs and prostitution was the anger and pain I felt after being gang raped at the age of nine. I did not choose to be a prostitute because I liked or wanted drugs. I was also not 'forced' into sex work. Some activist groups advocate that prostitution should be decriminalised because girls (and boys) are forced into this exploitation. But I feel strongly that we must recognise the social conditions that exist in our communities that support this type of exploitation. There were circumstances that led to my engagement in sex work and drugs, and I met these conditions *before* I was trafficked.

My mind flashes with ways of dealing with human trafficking. How could the traumatic events in my life have been avoided?

After I was abandoned by my guardians at the age of nine, I was raped by the members of a community gang. The community knew how the boys behaved, but did not act against them. Instead, they painted my mother's house in shame, which cast me out of the Khayelitsha community. I was pushed to live under the bridge in Cape Town with other street people. It was while I was trying to escape this life that I was then trafficked by someone I thought was a good friend when I arrived in Johannesburg. So my prostitution was never due to 'force', but to the social circumstances that make children like me ripe for exploitation.

My rape happened in the comforts of my community. My trafficking happened within the comfort of friendship. Violence against women works at all levels.

Being a prostitute and trafficked for sex work at a young age disrupts education, and leads to illiteracy and gaps in acquiring knowledge. My street life made me sound savvy, but writing articulately is a different skill.

Some people get annoyed with me because I am so honest about what really happens out there among prostitutes. In my advocacy work, I stand up for young girls who have been forced into sex work – that's my vision in life. There are ways to EXIT and stop this abuse, and it's up to individuals, civil society, institutions and government bodies to determine effective and long-range measures.

As a survivor, I feel that organisations working to eradicate human trafficking are bringing out more information about this societal scourge, but are not necessarily pushing for change at all political and social levels. I have been through several years of healing and understanding about the importance of exiting, but I realise that organisational managers themselves do not have the capacity to change the sex industry. It is the survivors who have the knowhow – they should be leading organisations and NGOs to push for and enforce dynamic change in the sex work industry. Organisations and governments are called upon to act forcefully and sustainably to eradicate the causes of this abuse.

There is a desperate need for the message to get out:

Stop human trafficking.

I'm writing this book because of the pain the prostitution cycle has caused me. As I deal with my own healing and the trauma that goes with it, I am seeing how change works in closing the wounds.

I am now advocating for women's rights and against the abuse of women and children. I'm doing this because once I woke up in a hospital bed after being beaten, drugged and enslaved. And I said to myself that for the rest of my life I would fight to make sure other girls did not go through what I experienced.

I want mothers to buy this book for their teenage daughters, fathers to buy it for their sons, friends to buy it for their girlfriends. Today I am Grizelda Grootboom, the name my mother gave me. Thank you for taking the time to get to know my story and find out who I am.

This work comes from my most inner being.

This must not be allowed to happen again.

For help call 08000 737283

Toll free national human trafficking helpline

Embrace Dignity

Since Grizelda walked into our office, we have been part of her incredible journey. She has also been an important part of our journey of the understanding the exploitation of trafficking and prostitution, and for this we are extremely grateful. We also wish to thank Grizelda for donating half the proceeds from the sales of this book to the ongoing work of Embrace Dignity in supporting 'Sisters' exiting sexual slavery and prostitution.

We wish to thank Carol Martin, social activist and retired educationist who recorded Grizelda's story and transcribed all the recordings, from which the final book was edited and published.

Thanks to our publisher.

Embrace Dignity can be contacted through our website
www.embracedignity.org.za